A Pictorial View of
the Last Century at
Wethered's Brewery

Pub sign from the short-lived Thomas Wethered pub in Rosoman Street, Clerkenwell, London.

A Pictorial View of
the Last Century at
Wethered's Brewery

Ray Evans

Best Wishes

Ray

Hudson and Pearson

Published by Hudson & Pearson Ltd. 2011

1 3 5 7 9 10 8 6 4 2

First published in Great Britain in 2011 by
Hudson & Pearson Ltd.

Hudson & Pearson Ltd.
Bradwood Works, Manchester Road, Dunnockshaw,
Burnley, Lancashire BB11 5PW

A CIP catalogue record for this book
is available from the British Library

ISBN 13 No. 978-0-9554017-6-3

Typeset by Hudson & Pearson Ltd.

Printed and bound in Great Britain by
Hudson & Pearson Ltd.
Dunnockshaw, Burnley, Lancashire BB11 5PW

Introduction

I worked at Wethered's for 27 years, mostly working in the garage. I have been collecting brewery photos for 35 years and most of the older photos are of transport. A few people had suggested it would be a good idea to write a book about Wethered's, so I thought I would do a little research on the history of the brewery, and also concentrate on the people who worked there and some of the events that took place.

During my time at the brewery there were some huge changes: five different fleets of lorries, the closing of the bottlery, a new warehouse and the new brewhouse extension to name just a few.

Like many other breweries, many of the employees stayed over 20 years and even onto 50 years. As you will discover when you read the book, the longest serving employees I can find are C H Yates, who worked there for 58 years as company secretary, and Ernest Baker for 56 years. Just about everybody who worked there thought it was a wonderful place to work, and the sports and social side at the brewery was excellent.

The photos not only cover the brewery and brewhouse, but also the vast sports and social side of the company. Many people in Marlow have often asked what the inside of the brewery was like; even some employees had never seen the inside of the brewhouse. With these photos you should get a feel for what it was like to work there and I have tried to cover as many different departments as possible and also feature as many employees as I can.

Nobody complained about working there; like many other breweries it was quite a family affair with many fathers, sons and brothers employed as well as a few marriages.

Then on to the closure, nobody really knows why the brewery closed as business seemed to be doing well and it was turning out some excellent beers. According to CAMRA one of the best bitters in England was brewed at Wethered's.

Ray Evans
August 2011

Acknowledgements

Jan Hoare   John Harris

Many thanks to the people below for photos or information, and to the Bucks Centre of Studies who keep the Wethered archives, and for putting up with us, it did seem a good opportunity to catch up with some sleep!

Beryl Evans
Ken Townsend
Mike Holland
Melvyn Deri
John Harris
Jan Hoare
Brewery History Society
Keith Osbourne – *label images*
Jeff Burke
Chris Malster
Lesley Tunney
Sheila Warne
Beryl Gillett
Chris Marlow

Michael Eagleton
Joan Bristow
Aubrey Jones
Brian Webb
Barbara Whitehead
Dennis Smith
John & Alma Austin
Mike Holliday
Mrs. Bellamy
Andy Ross
Sheila North
Tony Wilkinson
Ellen Webb

Andy Wilson
Joan & Rod Farrell
Ken Mansfield
Jenny Davies
Russell Davies
Nicky Pendlebury
Sid Prince
Ann Newsome
Pete Hogan
Linda Swadling
John Brainch
Joan Sykes
John (noj) Williamson

Contents

Like so many country firms, Wethered's regrettably never spent much time recording their history before they became a limited company. Thus, doubt is cast upon the exact date when beer was first brewed in the High Street.

There is one listing of 1758, but the most popular date is usually given as 1791 when the brewhouse and fermenting room were built. The building on the left, known as the "Old House" is thought to be built on the site referred to as being "formerly Miss Freeman's boarding school and the Three Tuns Tavern", a 16th century inn that housed the offices and board room. The firm was founded by George Wethered (1714 -1783). George married his first wife Elizabeth Gibbons whose father was a brewer in St Peter Street. In 1757, after the death of Elizabeth, he married his second wife, Anne Reynolds. On his death he bequeathed the malthouse, maltkiln, and yard to Thomas, his son by Anne. Thomas then leased it in 1788 from William Clayton for 99 years at £18 per annum.

There is no mention of a brewery until Thomas purchased the freehold in 1796 for £400 along with the new brewhouse, stables, and storehouses.

The building on the right is known as the "White House". It was leased to Thomas in 1791, and in 1820 Thomas purchased the freehold. It was not until George's death in 1783 that his son Thomas, in 1788, really founded the firm of Thomas Wethered where the brewery buildings now stand. Thomas' sons Owen and Lawrence became partners in the

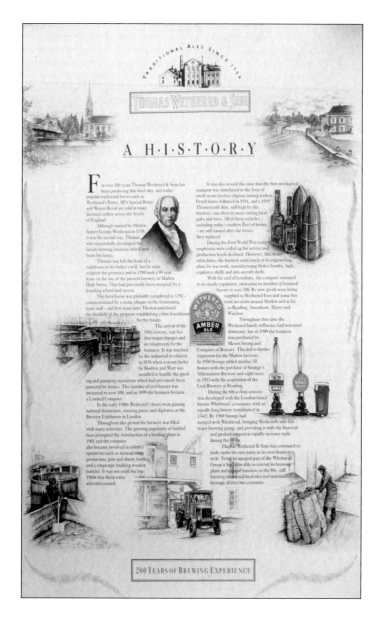

business and Thomas retired in 1845, living in Remnantz, West Street, Marlow, which he had purchased in about 1813, after it ceased to be a military college. He died in 1849.

1836 seems to be a turning point as a new Boulton and Watt boiler was installed, previous to this the power for various machines in the brewhouse and maltloft was provided by horses rotating a giant capstan.

In 1890, Owen Peel's sons, Francis and Walter, became partners and on Thomas Owen's retirement in the same year his son-in-law, John Danvers, took over. In 1899 the business became a limited liability company, with Owen Peel as Chairman.

Owen died in 1862, and, at an unconfirmed date, his sons, Thomas Owen Wethered of Seymour Court and Owen Peel Wethered, of the White House, became partners.

Their brother, Robert Peel Wethered, joined them in 1870, but he died just three years later.

Colonel F.E.Stevens was appointed general manager and at the same time Mr C.H. Yates was appointed secretary, a position he held until his death in 1935, following 58 years' service.

A huge expansion plan was put into place with the bottlery opening in 1901 and electric lighting plant being installed in 1903.

A brewhouse extension was built in 1905. Transport saw the introduction of steam engines and in 1911, petrol lorries.

In 1913, Wethered's took over Bird's Brewery, Reading with 9 licensed houses.

In 1914, the company won the Championship Gold Medal at the Brewers' exhibition plus 2 silver medals and 1 bronze.

With the outbreak of World War One in 1914, the company, doing their bit for the country, made thousands of stokes bombs and 18 pound shells.

1922-24 saw them win many prizes with their Thornycroft lorries.

In 1927, they took over William's Brewery, Wooburn, with 35 pubs bringing the total to over 200.

1926 saw the two Garton brothers, Richard and Charles, buy £82,000 worth of shares, along with Owen Henry Wethered who bought £20,000 worth of shares in the company to stop other brewers mounting a takeover.

1942: the death of Col.J.R. Wethered C.M.G D.S.O., aged 68 and the death of the chairman A S Garton in 1948. The brewery, in need of modernisation, merged with Strong's of Romsey in 1949. A year later, Strong's took over Strange's Brewery, Aldermaston with 50 pubs and then gave them to Wethered's, bringing their total to 232.

1958: double Centenary celebrations. Two garden parties were held for all the landlords and their wives.

1969: Whitbread took over Strong's and much modernisation was to come in the brewery and transport department.

Yet another brewhouse extension was built in 1984, but brewing only lasted another four years as 1988 was the last year of brewing. The premises carried on as a depot for another 5 years before finally closing on April 23rd 1993.

The poster (previous page), a history of the company, was framed and given out by the company to various people in the trade.

This regency style building above was known as The White House; Thomas Wethered acquired the freehold after it was leased for 30 years. Having a large garden, part of it was used to expand the brewery and that included the racking cellar. It is thought the bow windows and the bridge linking it to the old house were added at that time.

In 1921 a fire was caused by a wiring fault.

Francis Owen was living there up until his death in Tenerife in 1922, his widow Mrs Wethered then joined the board but died herself two years later.

Most of the time a member of the Wethered family would be living there, J R Wethered lived there in 1942 and when he died Mrs K D A Wethered was given permission to stay rent free.

Managing Director P.D.Power, whilst living in The White House in 1949, had jewellery and a fur coat stolen to the value of £700 by intruders who got in via the brewery yard and ransacked the upstairs rooms.

The ground floor in 1962 was converted into an off licence.

The White House is linked by a walkway to the Old House situated over the archway. The Old House was used for accommodation for the Head Brewer and Under Brewer who were offered a bedroom and sitting room. Terms included coal and gas in the sitting room, washing of table and bed linen, use of furniture and cooking. Mr and Mrs Rainbow were employed at a cost of 35/- per week to cook and attend to the two brewers and also to clean the offices on the understanding that the Head Brewer would repay the company monthly 8/10d and the Under Brewer 4/6d.

Sir Richard Garton O.B.E.

Charles Henry Garton

Above left: Sir Richard Garton O.B.E., Chairman, Chemist, Sugar Manufacturer and Brewing Director of Manbre and Garton Sugar Manufacturers. He was also chairman of brewers, Watney Combe Reid and a director of Lacon, Yarmouth, which was another brewery.

He first bought shares in Wethered's in 1918. A very busy man - another Chairmanship was of the British Empire Cancer Campaign. He was knighted in 1908. Garton had a stunning 3 year old race horse 'Sir Cosmo,' a top stallion at stud.

On his death in 1934, he left £2,641,364, that is equivalent to about £150 million today!

Above right is Charles Henry Garton, director from 1926 to 1934. Wethered's had the Gartons to thank for purchasing £82,000 worth of shares, thus rescuing it from a possible takeover from other brewers in London.

Arthur Stanley Garton J.P., *right,* was made a director upon the death of his father Charles, in 1934.

He became Managing Director in 1942, serving until his death in 1948.

Another very good rower, he competed in the 1909/10 and 11 winning Oxford crew in the University Boat Race. He was also a member of the winning Olympic eight crew at Stockholm in 1912.

A director of Marlow Water Company, and President of Marlow Rowing Club in 1939.

He was also Vice-President of Marlow Football, Hockey and Cricket Clubs.

Arthur Stanley Garton, J.P.

John Danvers Power

Three generations of Danvers Power:

John Danvers Power *(left)*
married into the Wethered family marrying
Edith Ethelston Wethered.
He was:
Partner 1890 -1899
Director 1899 -1916
Chairman 1922 -1927

Piers Danvers Power *(below left)* presenting Joe
Tubb with a tankard on his 50 year service.
A very informal meeting under the open dray
shed.
Piers was a director in 1921 and
Chairman 1942 - 1949

John Danvers Power *(below right)*
Director 1951 - 1956

Piers Danvers Power *(right)*

John Danvers Power

Born in Paris in 1854, Frank Erastus Stevens *(right)* was Managing Director from 1900 - 1926. He started with the company in 1899 on a salary of £77 per annum plus free use of the White House garden.

All employees had a half day holiday in 1924 in recognition of Col. Stevens' 25 years as general manager. He retired in 1926 with a pension of £500 per year.

The Chairman presented him with a testimonial album from the staff and employees and it was signed by everyone.

Col. Stevens died at his son's home in Bedfordshire in 1933.

Frank Erastus Stevens

Owen Francis Wethered *(left)*

Owen Francis Wethered *(left)* 1900 to 1981. A Commander in the Royal Navy he was a director from 1945 to 1949.

Seen here at Marlow Rowing Club with two navy personnel, the one in the centre being Theodore Lunnon.

Owen was the last Wethered to have an office at the brewery.

Left to right: Head brewer Paul Thompson, Arthur Coventry, H. H. Palmer, John Hodgkinson, Fred Jones and John Power, the Managing Director.

Horace Palmer was receiving his fifty year award in 1957. Although he retired at this point, he carried on as a company director. He had started in 1907, and having passed a satisfactory probation earned £15 per annum. After this ceremony and his retirement, John Hodgkinson took over the job as secretary.

Below right: Nigel Copeland – we have three secretaries on one page; Nigel took over from John Hodgkinson when John became Managing Director.

Below left: some of the office ladies with Horace. Peggy Angus, Sheila Warne, Horace, Hilda Saunders (a munitions girl), Arthur Coventry and Mrs. Attree.

Miss Lesley Payne, *far left,* Wethered Receptionist 'Telephone Operator' makes it through to the final six in the Whitbread News golden voice contest finishing third. Contestants were asked 20 questions, 15 of them testing the knowledge of the Whitbread Group. Prizes were given away by Ernest Marples, Postmaster General, who brought in postcodes and premium bonds and as Transport Minister introduced yellow lines, parking meters and seat belts.

The first office internal telephone was installed in 1917 at a cost of £18.10s 0d

It must have been quite a good place to work, as Linda Swadling *(lower left),* left and returned no less than five times.

The last receptionist was the larger than life, Carol Hart *(lower right),* who worked for Chiltern Inns, a department within the brewery.

Left: Paul (Hon Sec) Burdell, Secretary of Marlow Football Club and has done just about every job at the Club. Load planner, Glen North, with assistant transport manager, Melvyn Deri looking at the screen.

TELE SALES

Left to Right, Lynn Coll, Jan Smart – it looks like it's her birthday – Pearl White, Christine Humphries, Clare Lester, Jill Langley, and Daphne Armytage. *Inset:* Office Manager Robin Key.
The tele sales office was situated above the transport offices. These girls would take orders from landlords over the phone, whereas, years ago orders would be sent in by postcard.

The little truck below is from Dutton's Whitbread depot in Blackburn. It was originally a baker's van which then had the back removed and was used for promotional work and steam rallies. The number plate OBJ1 stands for "oh be joyful" the name of a Dutton's beer.

Left to Right: Dave Wooton, David Dean, Mick Wakefield and Fred Jolly. These four sneaked out of the transport office for a drink whilst Kelvin Gryckiewicz and the author were delivering Winter Royal to the Rose and Crown, Wooburn Green.

Back row: Daphne Armytage, Jan Smart, Pearl White, Diane Parsons, Carol Hobbs, Maggie Mercer.
Front row: Christine Humphries, Jill Langley, and Aileen Evans.

THE BETTER BREWED BITTERS

Two more of the lovely office girls modelling a new tee shirt. The town's church and brewery are featured on the shirt. Left: Managing Director's secretary, Fiona Houseman and cashier Sue Newman.

The slogan, subject of a company competition for employees, was won by carpenter John Harris, whose prize was a set of cut glass brandy glasses. At £1.35p a shirt, even in 1980 it was cheap.

Two Amber labels from the same era.

Les Tunney and Ann Provost, helping out the reps on a trade night at Slough Greyhound Track, the reps did many trade nights and these are just two of the attractive girls from the office brought along to try and drum up some business.

In front of the brewery, Herbert White is the taller of the two men. The two large windows, with Thomas Wethered etched at the bottom is now the site of Zizzi's restaurant.

These windows are now placed at the back of the restaurant. On either side of the pillars, two large brass signs are visible; the one on the right reads 'Thomas Wethered & Sons Brewers & Spirit Merchants'. The left one reads 'Agents to the Royal Exchange Assurance Fire Life Accident, Burglary, Employers Liability', they were brokers for the company.

Yes, the one on the right is blank! Bill Clark came out one morning with his polish, as he always did, but there it was – gone, never to be seen again!

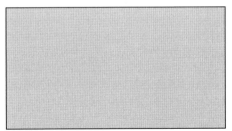

This is a much smaller name plate, *right,* that was put up later, and the picture of it has the reflection of a very attractive lady.

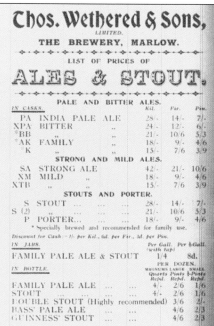

Thos. Wethered & Sons,
LIMITED.

THE BREWERY, MARLOW.

LIST OF PRICES OF

ALES & STOUT.

PALE AND BITTER ALES.	Kil.	Fir.	Pin.
IN CASKS.			
PA INDIA PALE ALE	28/-	14/-	7/-
XPA BITTER "	24/-	12/-	6/-
*BB "	21/-	10/6	5/3
*AK FAMILY "	18/-	9/-	4/6
*K " "	15/-	7/6	3/9
STRONG AND MILD ALES.			
SA STRONG ALE	42/-	21/-	10/6
XM MILD "	18/-	9/-	4/6
XTB " "	15/-	7/6	3/9
STOUTS AND PORTER.			
S STOUT	28/-	14/-	7/-
S (2) "	21/-	10/6	5/3
P PORTER...	18/-	9/-	4/6

* Specially brewed and recommended for family use.

Discount for Cash :— 1/- per Kil., 6d. per Fir., 3d. per Pin.

IN JARS.	Per Gall.	Per ½ Gall. (with tap)
FAMILY PALE ALE & STOUT	1/4	8d.

IN BOTTLE.	PER DOZEN. MAGNUMS LARGE SMALL Quarts Pints ½-Pints Rep'd. Rep'd. Rep'd.		
FAMILY PALE ALE ...	4/-	2/6	1/6
STOUT	4/-	2/6	1/6
DOUBLE STOUT (Highly recommended)	3/6	2/-	
BASS' PALE ALE	4/6	2/3	
GUINNESS' STOUT	4/6	2/3	

This is one of the earliest brewery photographs from the Victorian era, circa 1880, judging by the stove pipe hats. If you look carefully you can just about recognise the bricked up windows.

The original brewhouse, the fermentation room and the general office are behind these workers, and were built in 1791. Where the two barrels are standing, a brewhouse extension was put up in 1905 for £5,076.17s.0d.

This was another building completed by local builder Lovells. Everything seemed to coincide with the installation of electricity in 1903.

Between 1900 and 1920 the brewery was committed to spending large amounts of money on new boilers, bottlery and plant, along with steam.

Left: one of the earliest price lists, 1906.

This is the Head Brewer's office as seen looking down the yard from the High Street. It protrudes out from the wall and is now someone's bedroom. In 1880 it would have been used by head brewer Mr. S. Kirkpatrick. Before that, the job was in the hands of various partners in the business.

82,555. Beer, Ale, Wines, Spirits, and all other kinds of Fermented Liquors, Whiskey excluded. THOMAS WETHERED & SONS. Great Marlow, Bucks., Brewers, Spirit Merchants, and Mineral Water Manufacturers.— 21st November 1888.

The three legged vessel above was registered in November 1888 as a trade mark. The vessel which contained only a few gallons of beer would have been used in 1758 when brewing started in Marlow.

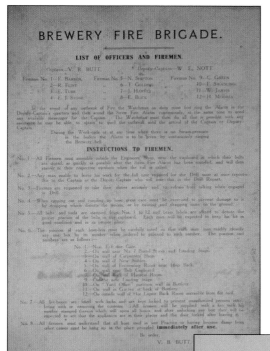

The brewery had their own fire brigade which was formed in 1909, being far quicker than waiting for the local brigade to couple up their horses to the tender.

This was not a rare thing in those days, as most large breweries and factories had their own brigade. The author can remember when he first started at the brewery, under the engineer's shop was a cellar known as No 13, and going down and seeing that all the pipes were perished and also saw that there was a drill book.

It would not take a genius to work out who was going to be captain of the fire brigade. Of course the job went to V.B. Butt, the Chief Engineer, who was paid 6d and the other men 3d per drill.

By the time the 1940's came, Butt had handed over the captaincy. His last signature was on June 5 1935. Now it was the turn of under brewer Paul Thompson to take over.

A carefully posed group of brewery workers, circa 1920, most are reasonably well dressed. Just visible in the background are two very smart ladies, looking as if they are waiting to be collected for an outing. The boys are most likely bottlery boys.

Brewery employment figures: there were 132 employees in 1913, this being the lowest number in recorded history. It was 55 less than in 1902, and 30 less than in 1899.

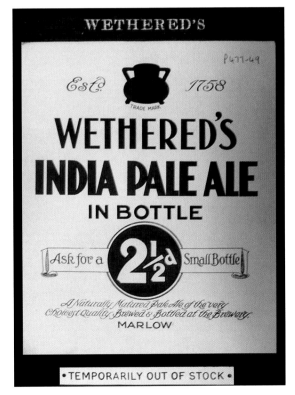

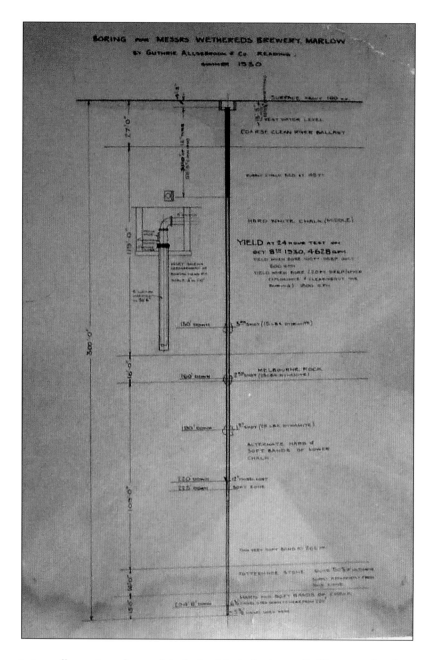

The artesian well was situated around the back of the boiler house. Drilling started in the summer of 1930. The well was originally only going to be 210ft deep. However, upon not finding any water they were considering using an air lift if the next test was not satisfactory. In the end they bored down to 300ft and finally finished in January 1931. In the hot summer of 1976, the brewers were getting very worried about the water level.

As can be seen on the certificate below, Rod Farrell was born at the brewery. As you enter from the High Street under the arch the building on the left is the one in which Rod and his mum, Jean, and dad, Andy, occupied. It is on the ground floor in between the two grey doors. Paul Thompson, the head brewer, occupied upstairs. Rod certainly had a big playground.

Rod Farrell's birth certificate

THE BREWERY COTTAGES IN OXFORD ROAD AND 'FRENCHIE THE BARBER'

Now we have seen where Rod lived, these cottages up on the right of Oxford Road are where at some time or another many of the employees lived.

However, there was one notable exception – Lou Chartier, known as 'Frenchie the Barber' whose salon was in West Street, next to the Three Tuns. Lou never worked at the brewery so how he managed to live there remains a mystery. The twelve cottages were built in 1902 by local builder Lovells for £3,000.

In the war a flying bomb damaged four houses, plus the Duke of Cambridge, the Royal Oak, and the Carpenters Arms.

Just lower down, another four cottages were agreed to be built in 1952. There was also a row of cottages at Farnham Common. Other tied houses were used where pubs had closed down.

Introduced mid 1930

Just under the archway from the High Street, this was a very busy yard with Bill Mudie and George 'Laddie' Levie conducting the traffic – a cavalcade of lorries, and with a big Guinness tanker waiting to go around the corner to unload. A Bedford, Seddon, and some Thornycrofts are also in view.

The Guinness tanker is parked on the weighbridge which was installed in 1928, for £515. This was the second one – the first had been built 60 years earlier.

When the Guinness tanker finally got around the corner he would pull alongside this building where these lorries are unloading to empty his tank, the contents of which would then be bottled – usually on a Friday.

In the corner of the picture below, a new toilet was built, and it was recommended to have a door which opened outwards. This was the idea of brewery head foreman Mr. W. Portlock as a method of keeping new boys from smoking and wasting time; impossible to put your foot up against it! Later, in the 1960's it became the Transport Office and after that it was the Signwriter's workshop.

Originally, these were horse drawn dray sheds being used here for sorting empty mineral cases. Situated behind the sheds was the greenhouse and garden. To the right of the photo is the mineral factory.

Right, this rare 1935 photo shows a horse drawn dray in the shed.

Below, is at the back of the mineral factory where the drivers would drive around and stack flagon cases in front of what was the original Wheelwright's shop. Shown here it is being used by the wine and spirit store. Beyond was the paddock for the horses.

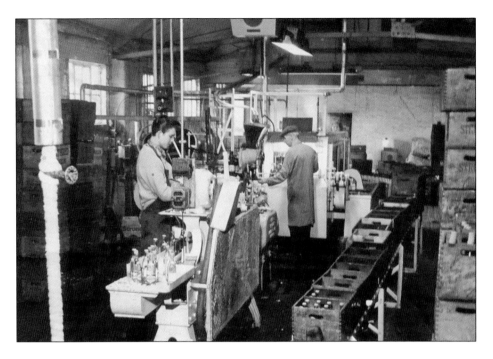

In the background is Fred Jones, another 50 year service man, and Monty's son, Tony Webb, is on the bottling line. Below are just some of the products that were bottled here.

A diploma and award for dry ginger ale resulted in W. Davis, Mineral Manager, receiving £5 on 15th November 1922

A single soda syphon filler, installed in 1928, was still in use in 1968.

The stables were converted to a mineral factory in 1934, with sliding doors and conveyors fitted at a cost of £1,648.

A lime green soda syphon, also in blue and brown.

This is the bottle store, built in 1960, located on what would have been Wethered's garden and lawn, upon which they held concerts and socials. Tommy Fee is in the middle checking the loads. The warehouse was moved again in August 1973 to the building that was once the wines and spirit store and also the paddock for horses.

THOMAS WETHERED & SONS LTD.

SOCIAL & CONCERT
at
THE WETHERED LAWN
on SATURDAY, AUGUST 30th, 1958
7 p.m. — Midnight

FREE BUFFET   LUCKY NUMBER...........107

1958 TICKET

Brian Bowles, driving a Hyster fork lift truck which was bought new in 1967 for £2,292.

Brian started in 1966 in the racking cellar, moved to the warehouse, and then on to the drays. He was the last driver to deliver from the brewery before it closed in 1993.

On a hot August day in 1973, these draymen have just returned to the brewery and are having a celebratory drink whilst waiting for Tony Wilkinson and the youngest of the office girls to cut the blue tape for the opening of the new warehouse. The draymen are sitting and leaning on the lorry which was hired. It was usual for the brewery to hire in the summer and at Christmas time. On the left, the driver and mate of the lorry with Brian Farrant, David 'Dixie' Dean, Mick 'Spud' Taylor, his brother Willie and John Llewellyn.

More workers, *below*, waiting for the tape to be cut: front office girls on the left, Bob Marrison, Fred Simmonds, Mick Mitchell, Tommy Fee and Eric Rollings.

This is the new warehouse nearing completion. The lorries are moving the beer cases up from the old warehouse to the new one completed in August 1973. Sadly, it was only to last 20 years.

Left, March 1984: sometimes there was more than beer stored in the warehouse. These two camels, featured in a Heineken advert, stayed for a couple of months before moving on to the West Country.

Label for a four pint plastic take home container.

Above is an 1836 date stone, and underneath, a water tank which was over the James Watt boiler house. This extension would have been added to house the boiler and extend the malt lofts.
It was erected by local builder William Bond at a cost of £1584.6s.2d and completed on December 31st. There are date stones all over the brewery buildings indicating when extensions were added.

Jim Hunter inscribed his name on the wall in 1966. Someone else has chalked that he was sacked, but the author and Jim know what really happened!

This is the oldest date stone, 1791. You will find it just through the archway from the High Street on the left hand side. Some say this is more likely to be the date the brewery first started.

This extension was built in 1983; the crane is installing six stainless steel fermenting vessels, and constructing the extension around them. The work was finished in 1984, enabling the brewing of other beers such as Whitbread Tankard, Sam Whitbread and Flowers Original Bitter.

Below, the opening ceremony for the extension.

The date stone about to be unveiled.

J. S. Kirkpatrick

J.S. Kirkpatrick, from Market Weighton, Yorkshire, was the first head brewer in 1880. Prior to that members of the family handled the brewing. When Kirkpatrick first started he was living at the same address as Gabriel Portlock, a stoker at the brewery in the High Street. Kirkpatrick's brother Charles was also an assistant brewer.

He rowed, as captain, with Charles Yates, secretary, in a four and were unbeaten during 1883 and 84. They were the winners of 7 challenge cups in one season.

On the death of Kirkpatrick in 1891, J. L. Holland took over the job of brewer. He also lived at the same address as an employee, a brewer's clerk Thomas Stanmore, at 80, High Street. Number 78 next door was reputed to be the last house in Marlow to have electricity connected. It was occupied by Mrs. Jarvis whose late husband was the cooper. Holland spent 29 years as the brewer, and was made a director in 1917.

The company presented him with a handsome silver salver for winning a championship gold medal, two first prizes (silver medals), and a third diploma, all for beers he brewed from 1891 to 1915. He died in Saltash, Cornwall aged 69.

When second brewer Parkhurst left, Arthur V Greenstreet was engaged on the recommendation of Sir Richard Garton and started on £275 per annum. He was the brother of actor Sidney Greenstreet.

Thomas Wickham Story

Eustace Nigel Crew took over after the death of Holland in 1920 and Belgian Monsieur Simonart, a war time substitute brewer, was released. E. N. Crew was granted £30 for inspection of French Breweries, he also won 17 prizes at brewery exhibitions for his beers, in the short time in charge he also remodelled the bottlery.

C.T. Foulsham took over upon Crew's death, after being his understudy, and Walmsley was appointed as second brewer. However, Foulsham left in 1937 after being with the company for eighteen years.

Paul Thompson

In 1939, Thomas Wickham Story resigned after just two years following an issue concerning a Rolls Royce, but still managed to win two Diplomes D Excellance at the International Exhibition. Story was from Harrogate and was only 42 when he died in 1943.

R. Nobile, another Head Brewer arrived from Arkell's Brewery, Swindon in September 1939 and moved on to Shanklin Brewery, Isle of Wight in 1951 with references from Strong's Directors saying 'excellent brewer whilst at Wethereds'.

Second brewers tend to come and go on a regular basis. E.A Essex moved on in 1945 to Meux's Brewery. W.W. Edwards started but soon left, and that made way for Paul Thompson, who started as under brewer in 1947 and succeeded Nobile as Head Brewer.

Mike Gregory

Mike Gregory took over from Thompson and he came from Romsey Brewery. He spent a few years as brewer then went on to become Managing Director in September 1961. On his departure he took over the family hotel - the Mermaid at Rye in Sussex.

I. D. Wilson

Bill Fisher

Lance Ogden

Howard Smith

Bernard Scott

I. D. Wilson who was temporary Head Brewer from Strong's of Romsey, after Mike Gregory and before Bill Fisher.

Bill Fisher started 1 Sept 1962, with I. D. Wilson returning to Romsey. Neil Binnie became second brewer, and then moved on to Phipps' Brewery with Jim Nowell taking over as second brewer.

Jim Nowell   1973 - 75

Dan Tomason, from Eldridge Pope, 1975

Lance Ogden brewed the famous Winter Royal for the Queen's Jubilee. He left in May 1979 to go to Castle Eden. Second Brewer Alan Griffiths also left, going to Samlesbury.

Howard Smith started on 16 May 1979.

Bernard Scott, the last brewer, came from Leney's of Wateringbury, Kent in 1982 and stayed until the brewing ceased in 1988.

Here, Jack Cook is being presented with a glass of Silver Jubilee Ale by head brewer Lance Ogden, with 2nd Brewer Alan Griffiths looking on. Queen's Silver Jubilee Ale was first brewed on 1st March 1977 and distributed throughout the Whitbread chain.

It was then decided to produce it on draught in the winter and give it the famous name, Winter Royal. When Wethered's closed it continued to be brewed at Cheltenham, then at McMullen's, and onto Gales of Horndean, finally being brewed at Castle Eden, County Durham. The Castle Eden brew was the closest it ever came to the true Wethered's Winter Royal taste, probably because Lance went there as Head Brewer. Lance wore steel tips on his shoes just to warn people he was coming, for example to the sample room! With Winter Royal's original gravity of 1056 you didn't need too many!

"Advance" shown above, at the top of Marlow High Street. Another excuse for closing the brewery was the size of the lorries using Marlow High Street, but having driven up and down the High Street many times myself in this lorry I never had a problem. Also, lorries of this size are still using the High Street. Seen leaning on his bike is Len Roblett who for many years was Marlow Football Club's most vocal and lively supporter!

In the photo below, do these three know something we don't? Not a smile between them! They are looking at a model of a proposed new depot which was built at Wooburn, but anyone who went

to see the depot knew it would be far too small. The fact that the yard didn't have enough room to turn round a 42 foot articulated lorry was made worse when it was discovered that junction 3 of the M40, the planned access point for the depot's lorries, was a restricted junction. The restriction in this case being the only way on to it was East towards London, and the only way off it was from London; a big disadvantage to any transport operation with most of its customers to the West. Needless to say it never opened as a Whitbread depot.

From left, Keith Budd, John Whittaker – Whitbread Regional Manager – and Tony Wilkinson.

THE **REAL** WETHEREDS FORECAST

DRY
DULL
&
GLOOMY

WETHEREDS
BREWERY WILL
CLOSE IN MAY

THE BEER
WILL NEVER
BE THE SAME

JOIN THE MARCH AGAINST CLOSURE

ASSEMBLE OUTSIDE **THE MARLOW DONKEY PUB**
(Opposite Marlow British Rail Station)

SATURDAY 26th MARCH - Starting 12 NOON.

"One last chance", this advertisement appeared in the CAMRA newspaper recruiting members for a protest march from the Marlow Donkey pub to the brewery. Once the brewers made a decision to close any of their breweries they stuck to it. They were never going to change their mind but at least CAMRA gave it a go.

Police Escort: Demonstrators make their way along Marlow High Street en route to Wethered's Brewery.

Hey Mr Tambourine Man!: A lighter hearted moment is added to the sombre occasion by a jazz band, which led the marchers through the Buckinghamshire town.

Installed in 1960 for £1,869.11s, the mill, top, crushes the grist which is then sent down to the mash tun.

Peter Castree seen here oiling the mill in the mid 1960's.

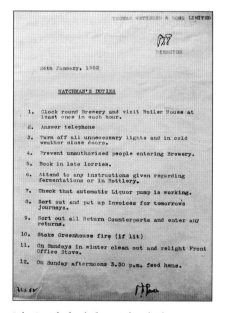

Like I said, don't forget the chickens.

Alf 'Jock' Irvine, starting at 6am, tipping sacks of malt known as grist into the hopper. This is at the top of the brewhouse.

Jocks domain! – When asked about the lack of excitement in his job, Jock said that he had seen enough excitement when he landed at the beach on D Day!

Just in case he forgot there was a chalkboard on the left.

In 1907, Head Brewer, J.L. Holland reported the loss of beer on the evening of 22 August. George Wicks, head coolerman, lost 14 barrels of Mild Ale by running the refrigerator over which he also did on 4 July the year before. 7 barrels went to waste on 22 July 1904 caused by leaving the tap of No. 7 fermenting vessel open.

Mr F. O. Wethered gave instructions to dismiss him at once, which the head brewer did.

The brewhouse was just a maze of small rooms for storing malt. Here are just two of them, all had wooden floors.

In 1907 Wethereds were enquiring about lager from Allsopp's.

In 1917 the M.D. reported loss of beer amounting to £4.5s.9d due to a mistake on part of H. Stacey, a "war time copperman"

1942: Xmas Day was a holiday; although back to work on Boxing Day you could go home when no longer required.

Brewing ceased on 11 Feb. 1947 due to a cut back on electricity caused by the national coal shortage, re-started 3rd March.

In 1948 the brewery increased the employees' holiday from one week to two.

A loss of 15 barrels of AA and 18 barrels of XXX was caused by brine leaking into the coils of the tanks, having been soldered instead of brazed.

Number 1 mash tun, where hot liquor was poured over the grains. On the bottom is a double layer of brass plates with slots so that the liquor can run through to the undervat.

In 1938 most of the brewing was done at night.

Mash tuns 1 and 2

Ian 'Ginger' Irvine and Bob 'Pitbull' Pitwell checking the mash.

When the liquor has drained through, and left for an hour or so, the spent grains have to be thrown out by hand, so two brewhouse workers would don their tee shirts, shorts and wellies and throw it through an open door into a trailer in the alley below.

Ceramic advertising plaque

For years, two men would throw the grains out of the mash tun and through a door into the trailer below.

As in the photo on the left, in later years grains came down a chute as it only needed one man to shovel it down a hole in the bottom of the mash tun.

Henry Bowles who worked for local farmer 'Babe' Lee would take the trailer to the farm for cattle feed.

Trailer below collecting spent hops.

Jock stripped to the waist shovelling out the grains

The hot liquor running down from the mash tun is now referred to as wort (liquid extracted from the mashing process) picture above show the taps, open, filling the copper trough prior to being pumped up to the copper. On the wall behind there was a box with a small sample glass in it.

Harry 'Boxer' Silver worked here in the 1960's and 1970's. The samples he provided were very malty!

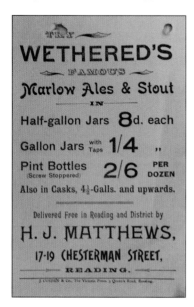

TRY

WETHERED'S

— FAMOUS —

Marlow Ales & Stout

—IN—

Half-gallon Jars **8**d. each

Gallon Jars with Taps **1/4** ,,

Pint Bottles (Screw Stoppered) **2/6** PER DOZEN

Also in Casks, 4½-Galls. and upwards.

Delivered Free in Reading and District by

H. J. MATTHEWS,

17-19 CHESTERMAN STREET,

— READING. —

At the end of the boil, the wort was dropped into the whirlpool. As its name suggests, it operates through centrifugal forces that rotate the wort at a very high speed forcing unwanted solids (trub), proteins and residue of the hops into a cone in the middle of the whirlpool. The wort was then left in the whirlpool for an hour before the wort runner began to transfer to the fv's.

The picture below shows the hop pocket (sacks). The majority of the hops were from Kent as the writing on the pockets show, a stock of 8 weeks was the norm. The hop pockets in large sacks were last used in May 1978, eventually coming in pellet form, a blow to the draymen who used to make them into aprons.

Coal cellar.

When the wort had finished running through, it would be pumped up to the coppers where it would be boiled.

This one was originally coal fired and was converted in 1910 to being steam heated. The coal would be hauled up from the cellar below through a hole in the floor; the heaters for the two coppers cost £250 and were fitted by Worssam.

This copper is referred to as the 'new copper' which was installed in 1962, at a cost of £5,945, by the biggest crane in Europe; it even made the BBC news bulletins! This is the stage where the hops are added. Peter Winterbourne can be seen adding hops which are in pellet form.

Jan is standing by the old system whereby the beer is pumped through copper pipes. Water runs over the top to cool the beer then it is pumped into the fermenting vessels to ferment.

Left is the much smaller replacement stainless steel paraflow, installed in 1971.

This picture gives a view of the tun room showing some of the many varied sized fermenting vessels situated in the block. This was unusual as most other breweries had their fv's set in a more uniform layout, mostly the same size and in rows for ease of access when running the wort to them etc.

The reason for this is probably that parts of the brewery were added on at various times over the years. The stairs in the picture below were to the tower that was built in 1905 to house the heat exchanger.

During the boom times of the 1980's, Wethered's Bitter, S.P.A. and Winter Royal were marketed to Whitbread London and the Home Counties tied houses as well as locally.

A new tun room was added with 6 new stainless steel fv's giving a further 1200 barrel capacity. The picture also shows the yeast bins where the wort was added to be stirred into smooth slurry and then tipped in to the fv to start the fermenting process. The hoist that was used to bring the bins up from the yeast room can also be seen.

Left: Ian Irvine and Melvyn Deri, pitching the yeast in the new fermenting vessels.

Top picture, looks like porridge, but it is yeast forming while fermentation takes place.

Left, adjustable temperators and adjustable skimming boat.

Howard Smith, the head brewer, far right, showing some visitors around the fermentation room. As you can see the yeast has dropped and is well into the fermenting process. You can also see Howard inspecting the sacks of malt.

Below a 1980's bar towel – a very limited selection of Wethered Bar Towels were made.

No. 8 was new in 1907; it is the small one on the right and was mainly used for Mild and other small brews.

1913: An extra floor was fitted in the brewhouse for more storage.

1917: The M.D. reported that owing to the great shortage of Mild beer the brewing of stout, the sale of F.P.A and stout in pints should be discontinued.

1919: Brewing stout was resumed. Gravity at 1042 retailed at 7d a pint.

In 1921 the wood of No.1 fermenting vessel – the largest vessel in the tun room, was found to be rotten and had to be replaced, at a cost of £132.10s.0d

You are not seeing things – in the photo above there is no copper lining to these vessels, the photo was taken after the scrap men came in 1988.

They agreed to brew Coronation Old Draught beer retailing at 1/6d a pint in 1953.

Agreed to put XXX on draught for the winter months in the public bars at 1/5d a pint in 1953.

Coins below were struck from the copper lining of fv 1 which contained the final brew of Wethered's Bitter on 18 April 1988.

After the yeast was skimmed from the brew it was forced through a press using compressed air. This process returned any beer out of the yeast, leaving it as a dry cake. This was knocked into trays and then stored in the refrigerator for future brews. The picture shows the yeast man Melvyn Deri doing this, any spare yeast was collected to use in the making of Marmite.

Sid Huddleston, the last cooper, started work on 2nd January 1947. His wages were £7.5s.0d. A decline in draught beer in 1954 saw conversion of 200 barrels (36 gallons per barrel) into kilns (18 gallons). The last wooden barrels were withdrawn in June 1972. It must have been heart breaking for Sid to have to cut them in half for use as flower tubs, Sid's workshop was at the back of the cask washing shed. In 1938 they purchased 150 Kilns at £2.0s.0d. each, 200 firkins at £1.5s.6d. and 50 pins at 17/6d.

Reg. Lewis.
Reg also worked in the cask shed, always wore a beret and walked with a slight limp.

This cask shed was built at the end of September 1902. Also at this time a 7ft wall was erected behind the cask shed.

Head Brewer Howard Smith putting on a test barrel and checking it carefully for cleanliness.

Dennis Winterbourne checking the barrels with a light and a sharp rod to get out any foreign objects.

John Bond and Bill Gutteridge filling wooden barrels in the 1950's.

The racking was later moved around the corner. Here *(left)* is Colin Budd filling metal casks in the 1980's. The last day of racking was 26 April 1988.

Whitbread changed the name of Wethered's Bitter to Trophy and then back to Wethered's Bitter.

Finally onto the loading stage: the draymen here are loading wooden barrels onto the drays.

Advertising board – someone has been using it as a dartboard!

Drayman, Fred Willis 18½ years' service.

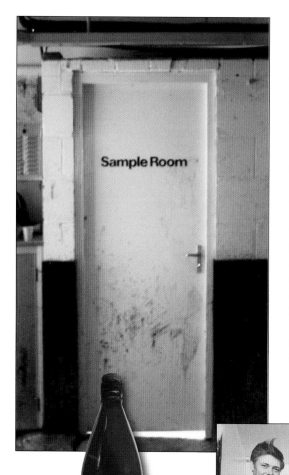

The allowance in 1910 was as follows: men – 3 horns or 3 bottles of ginger beer, boys – 3 bottles of ginger beer, no part of the allowance was to be taken away from the brewery except by draymen. It was issued only in the mess room at 6am, 11am, 1pm, 4pm and 6pm.

Beer allowance in the 1960's was given out daily at 7.30am and again at 3.45 pm, you had to take your own quart bottle which you paid 6d for.

Many had a case with four bottles, they would fill up morning and afternoon. For many years it was Mild Ale then the management relented and changed to bitter plus a bottle of lemonade, there were plenty of takers for a pint at 7 30 a.m.

The Sample room moved about 2 or 3 times but the author always seemed to find the key!

Roger 'Splodge' Young, Eddie Tilbury, Peter Winterbourne and, Head Brewer, Bernard Scott. The photo was taken in 1983, in the sample room in the cellar. This was another promotion for Winter Royal.

Head Brewer, Bernard Scott looked after his brew house staff by taking them on outings, and giving Christmas parties. This one, being the last, was held in the engineer's workshop on Christmas Eve 1987. On this occasion there were quite a few guests, including Wilkie, Carol Woodley from the free trade shop, and receptionist Jill Regan.

… Other faces you might recognise.

A few more below.

GYLE COLLECTION AND FERMENTATION RECORD

LAST BREW

GYLE NUMBER 299							DATE BREWED 18/4/88				
FV	TYPE	EXPECTED BRLS	DIP 1ST COP	DIP 2ND COP	DIP LIQUOR	EST DIP FINISH	TEMP	GRAVITY	FINISH DIP	LITRES	BRLS
9	SPA	84	140	54	–	–	66	40·4	60·6	1384	80·5
12	WB	90	144	75	42	42	66	35·4	52·8	1382·7	84·5
1	WB	190	217	130	90	90	66	35·5	108·8	2844·3	173·8

All Filterate 6 FV9 for filling 80 LL AFT on Mon 25/4

FV NO: 9				TYPE SPA	FV NO: 12				TYPE WB	FV NO: 1			FV NO: WB
Date	Time	Temp	Gravity	Remarks	Date	Time	Temp	Gravity	Remarks	Date	Time	Temp	Gravity	Remarks
18/4	E4	66	40·4		18/4	E4	66	35·4		18/4	E4	66	35·5	

Date Racked _____
Dip at Back _____

The effect that the coming beer orders would have on the industry, the changing markets for real ale, and the local objections to a busy brewery in the town centre (council labelled it a badly sited user) brought about a decision by Whitbread to close the brewery in 1988. The distribution side stayed on for another 5 years, finally closing in 1993. The picture shows the brewing sheet for the last ever brew at Wethered's. The beer brewed on the 18th of April 1988 was Special Pale Ale (SPA) and Wethered's Bitter which was brewed in fv1; this brought to an end a brewing tradition that had started in 1758.

As the demand grew for bottled beers Wethered's decided to expand and move on from bottling by hand and to build a bottling store with machinery. This was built for £800 in 1901.

A new bottling machine was installed in 1904 - a Hayward Tyler costing £15.15s.0d. However, it was not too long before that was replaced by a Eureka 12 bottle filler.

As the demand grew, 12,100 barrels in 1910 had risen to 14,362 in 1912, which prompted a further upgrade to an 18 head filler costing £220.

The trade in bottled beers was then mostly in quart size bottles (61%) amounting to 12,345 barrels - 185,412 dozen bottles. Bottled beer now formed one third of the brewery total trade.

A short list of casualties, not a safe place to work!

1904: A boy, Charles Grant, had a deep cut by his eye caused by flying glass whilst labelling only six yards away from the filler, another boy T. Coster had a very deep cut on his palm, which resulted in a visit by the government inspector.

The boy, Herbert Allen had his left eye destroyed by glass whilst standing near one of the bottling machines, and was sent at once by train to Reading Hospital but unfortunately had to have his eye removed.

George Frith (son of the head cask washer) and employed in the bottlery, drowned whilst bathing in the river in his dinner hour.

1912: It was reported that Ernest Barker met with an accident which resulted in him losing his left arm; he later received compensation of £225, equivalent of £14,000 today.

Women can be seen working here; they were first employed in 1913. In that year there were 13 women and 8 boys employed. They employed women instead of boys because the boys were noisy.

Breakages became expensive and excessive. In 1914, the women were given a milk allowance providing their wages stayed the same. Starting times for the women changed in 1938 from 6am to 7.30am.

The boys were very quick and nippy, but had a reputation for being rough, dirty and careless; however they worked hard for small wages. Boys could start work at 6am, 6 days a week - something the women were unable to do.

There was unlimited overtime for boys over 18, they frequently worked until midnight.

H. Stacey, G. Latham and R. Stroud were dismissed in 1909 with one week's pay. However all other boys' wages were increased.

Here are two attractive circular beer labels, probably used on quart bottles. Audit Ale was a very strong beer which a number of breweries produced for Oxford and Cambridge Colleges.

The photo above was taken from The Bucks Free Press, at the back of the bottling hall. The two girls seated are putting labels on by hand.

The Free Press reported that at the brewery "one walks through a labyrinth of mash tuns, coppers and pipes, the gleaming surfaces of the huge copper vessels are evidence of cleanliness."

They had an employee to clean the architect's motor bike for 6d and on a Sunday someone would sweep the yard for 6d.

In one corner of the bottling hall there was an iron ladder coming up from the cellar. In 1915 considerable pilfering was found to be taking place and an iron gate was erected over the cellar entrance along with corrugated partitions, at a cost of £40.

Little Doris Bettle is operating the liquid carbonic bottling machine. This had been bought in 1938 for £1,550. Nelly Davison at the back, stands in front of the1950 liquid bottle washer bought for £6,270.

Jan, with Rita Hillsdon (showing a bit of leg!) operating the 40 head Worssam filler. This had been ordered in 1947 for £4,302.15s.0d., it was usually used on Mondays, Tuesdays and Wednesdays, for what were called 'our own beers' – Light Ale, Brown, Amber and Special.

Sheila Goode and Stella Stroud are feeding bottles into the back of this Dawson bottle washer installed in the early 1960's.

A semi-automatic decrating machine fitted in 1968, which needed just one person to operate it.

Kitty Hoare on the labeller, with Margaret filling crates alongside Peter Simmonds. A Banks labeller was bought in 1951 to be used for Guinness, Bass and Worthington.

Estimates for printing labels from 29 March 1913:

1,000,000 large Family Pale Ale

1,000,000 small

1,000,000 large Stout

1,000,000 small

1,000,000 Oatmeal Stout

Results of tenders for printing and paper:

Wellbourne and Simpson of Marlow   £177.1s. 8d

Hobbs of Maidstone   £171.17s.6d

These are just two examples.

Embossed labels introduced in 1946.

Last day of bottling took place on 26 March 1971, Amber being the last beer to be bottled. It resulted in the loss of jobs of four women and two men.

Gladys Deane and Ray Anson are filling crates which would then be sent down on the conveyer to the warehouse. This would be a Thursday or Friday as the bottles are coming from the left hand conveyer being filled from the liquid bottling machine. They only used the machine on those days for bottling Bass, Worthington and Guinness. Loads would be made up in the warehouse then sent on to the brewery's many outlets.

The Pulloxhill label was brewed to raise money for the church tower fund and sold as Pulloxhill Church Ale. Also, a very nice cider label, bottled for William Evans of Hereford.

Yes it's that man Jan again, this time oiling parts on the chilling plant. The ammonia filled plant was used for chilling the beer in the tank rooms; the plant was situated in the cellar of the bottling hall. Sometimes the ammonia would leak from the gland of the pump, and then it was time for a gas mask.

Radox beer storage tanks. When they were taken out it was used as the carpenters' shop.

Tank room next to the bottling hall

This photograph was taken on the loading stage by the bottlery, most of these men are charge hands from several departments of the brewery *Back row:* unknown, Tommy Golding, unknown, unknown. *Mliddle row:* unknown, Stan Coker, Swadling, unknown, Harry Hillsdon. *Front row:* Alf Alldous, George Levie, unknown.

Local man Bob Eyres in the middle, the other two are casual workers. The brewery used to take on casual workers at busy times, usually employed from the R A F and Army whilst on leave.

This photo was taken outside the Marquis of Granby, Cemetery Junction, Reading in about 1900. In later years the upstairs was used as a gym for boxers. Plenty of big drinkers in those days - the amount the barrels held was 36 gallons!

There were two classes of draymen - Town and Country. However, there only seems to have been two drayman for the town, the rest being country draymen. The draymen were all paid the same wage in 1887, 14/- (70 pence) a week. Wages in 1920 were 50/-; Mr. Sloan and those in charge of the horses received 70/-.

In 1911 five horses were bought during the year, George and Mary, a handsome pair of black horses who were looked after by Mr. Sloan. One horse 'Lieutenant' was taken by the War Department, but the brewery received a £55 subsidy.

In 1915 the draymen and their horses were:

W Herbert	'Major' & 'Captain'
W Didcock	'Lancer'
F Wye	'Bugler'
J Shipton	'Dragoon'
Job Jones	'Boxer' & 'Mary'
S Harris	Tom'

J. Lovegrove and W. New of the horse feed department were dismissed for stealing beer from the fermenting vessels.

Late 1890'S, brewery dray delivering to the White Lion, Marlow and opposite was the Red Lion. Next door to the White Lion on Quoiting Square housed A.J. East's second-hand furniture store which was later taken over by Platt's Garage.

All the horses were given names, some of the earliest:
1849:
Pedler' bought for £42.
'Violet' - £35
'Flower' - £37
'Dolly' - £36
'Tom' - £31.10s

A few more names…. 'Captain', 'Prince', 'Duke', 'Turpin', 'Snowden', 'Drayton', 'Boxer' 'Spark', 'Blackbird' and 'Taffy'.

1860: Others listed were 'Judge', 'Keen', 'Grove', 'Vicker' and 'Wilkens'.

Sadly there were a few deaths; in 1848 'Dumpling' was killed on Wycombe Hill. Two died in 1888 - 'Champion', on Hedsor Hill and 'Trooper' at Clewer, Near Windsor.

In addition to buying horses, the brewery also sold various horses: 7 were sold in 1877, 9 in 1878, 11 in 1880 and 10 in 1886.

Besides naming the horses, they also numbered them. By 1895, they had gone through 410 horses which were costing £60 each, the average age of the horses bought was between 5-7 years old and some were kept on until they were 20 years old.

In 1894 3 died of arsenic poisoning. In 1912 there were a total of 19 horses, one being sold at the Marlow Fair. The total now down to 18 due to the gradual introduction of motorised transport.

Question: what is a line up of prize winning lorries doing in this picture titled 'Stable Block'? Answer: behind the lorries is the stable block which was built in 1899 and stabled 32 horses.

The cost was £1,414.10s.7d. (Always down to the last penny!) In later years it was turned into the mineral water factory. Left hand side of the stable was the Wheelwrights' shop. There was a new dray shed erected in 1900 at a cost of £134.4s.7d.

The above photo was taken by one of Marlow's best known photographers, Norman Greville, who had his business, not far from the brewery entrance, at number 62 High Street.

This picture of Norman also appeared in "A Fifth Trip Back In Time" compiled by the author of this book along with Michael Eagleton.

You will recognise the Hare & Hounds at the bottom of Redpits Hill Marlow. Pictured with the landlord and his wife are draymen, Rockall & Joby Jones. The photo was taken in the late 1930's, note the horses' hats! It seems like in 1938 these were the last two remaining horses left.

A statement from the Managing Director read, "Our two heavy horses in poor health both were put down. We received £4 each for the carcasses, one of them had an enlarged liver & fatty heart condition and were put down on the advice of our vet."

They were then going to purchase two Suffolks but changed their minds.

While Major F.O. Wethered was at camp the brewery did not charge for 'Tommy' the horse or his groom.

In 1903 Gray's shop, on the corner of Institute Road and opposite the brewery entrance, was damaged when a horse was frightened by a car. It was probably the first car the horse had seen!

No action was taken by the shop.

Joby Jones, probably the last horse drawn drayman.

'Firefly' was the second steam engine to be bought. Since all the horses were given names, they carried on the tradition by naming the steam engines.

This is the christening of 'Firefly' on 26 August 1905 carried out by five year old Adeline Wethered, who was granddaughter of the chairman, Owen Peel Wethered *(far right)*. Adeline's twin brother Owen (next to her in a sailor suit) was a director of the company from 1945 to 1949. Victor Butt is in the driving seat, and the building behind was the harness room.

The brewery had a total of five steam tractors:

'Togo' – Reg. No. AA 2030 delivered June 1905   (Wallis & Stevens)

'Firefly' - AA 2046 - August 1905 – (Wallis & Stevens)

'Dragon' - AA 2079 – November 1905 – (Wallis & Stevens)

'Onward' - D 2587 - May 1906 - (Aveling & Porter)

'Forward' - D 3085 - March 1907 - (Aveling & Porter)

Wallis and Stevens' engines were bought for £ 416 each

Aveling and Porter engines were bought for £ 450 each

Thought to be Ye Butchers Arms, Hoisier Sreet, Reading. There were usually three men to a traction engine so where the rest have come from is a good question. It is interesting that there is no brass name plate yet, just a name written on the headboard. A well loaded trailer – a ladder would be required.

Eight trailers were supplied new in 1907 by Couchman, Victoria Road, Marlow for £80 each. Wallis and Stevens also supplied trailers for the same price.

1906: Authorised to engage another blacksmith if necessary in view of extra work entailed by traction engines.

When taking trailers over Marlow Bridge, the steam engine crew would have to unhook the trailer and a team of horses would take the trailer over and recouple, then off they would go, the reverse happening when coming home. However, in 1910 with the invention of the telephone, the draymen were able to phone the brewery office from the bottom of Bisham Hill for them to send the horses down to the bridge to bring the trailer over, thus saving a lot of time.

Wethered's granted the sum of £2.2s.0d towards the cost of tarmac through Bisham village in 1907.

The Aylesbury town clerk, in 1909, sent his thanks to the company for the prompt and efficient help by employees for recovering a heavy motor after breaking decking on Marlow Bridge.

How Marlow Bridge looked in 1910.

MARLOW BRIDGE AND HEAVY MOTOR TRACTION.

Thomas Lowe, of 12, Chalk Pit-cottages, Marlow, for whom Mr. Shone, solicitor, Marlow, appeared, was summoned for having obstructed the highway at Bisham, on the 24th September, by leaving a motor-trailer thereon.

He pleaded not guilty.

P.C. Rhodes stated that he was on duty on the Marlow-road, Bisham, at about 2 o'clock, when he saw defendant in charge of a heavy motor-engine with trailer attached pull to the near side of the road at Marlow Bridge. He remained there some few minutes and then left and went into Marlow, after detaching the trailer—a heavy waggon—and leaving it behind. About twenty minutes later the trailer was removed by two horses. It was at the narrowest part of the Bisham-road where the trailer pulled in. It was necessary that the trailer should be detached as the load over Marlow Bridge must not exceed five tons, but it was usual on such occasions to have a couple of horses ready to convey the trailer across.

Cross-examined, witness did not agree that the width of the road was 18ft. 6ins.; it was about 17ft. He did not take in the gutter in the measurement, because the trailer was not brought into the gutter. The trailer followed the motor as soon as it could. There was only just room for a vehicle to pass.

Mr. Shone, for the defence, said that the bye-law provided that a locomotive should not remain stationary for a longer period than 20 minutes. In this case this time had not been exceeded, and he thought that a reasonable time. Further evidence was unnecessary.

The Magistrates considered that Mr. Shone must proceed with his case.

Mr. Shone: Then the case being of great importance to us I wish formal notice taken of my objection to the proceedings going any further. My point is that that terminates the case. There has been no evidence of obstruction.

Proceeding, Mr. Shone said it would be impossible to convey the trailer away more quickly. There was a standing regulation at the brewery which stated that the moment a motor with trailer attached arrived at Marlow Bridge a signal was at once sent to the Brewery and horses were despatched and the trailer removed with the least possible delay.

Defendant, sworn, said that on the outward journey it was the custom to take a part of the load over the bridge and then the requisite amount was afterwards added. On the homeward journey it was usual to proceed over the bridge first with the engine and the trailer would follow in charge of two horses with as little delay as possible. This happened on the day in question and no delay at all took place.

Sir H. Vansittart-Neale: Are the regulations always complied with?

Defendant: Yes, Sir.

Arthur John Cripps, assistant driver, who was in company with the last witness at the time, corroborated his evidence, and added that he went to the yard immediately they got to Marlow Bridge and found, as is always the case, the horses ready harnessed and they were at once taken to the bridge and conveyed the trailer to the yard.

The above-mentioned regulations, a copy of which was handed the Magistrates, were sworn to by the yard-foreman at Messrs. Wethered's, by whom defendant is employed. The horses, he said, were always kept ready and were sent off immediately a trailer arrived.

This concluded the evidence, and after retirement the Magistrates dismissed the case.

One of Wethered's traction engines, probably 'Togo', tipped over whilst delivering. As was usual at the time, everybody was very keen to get in the picture, including a young chap in a Borlase School cap close to the wheel.

Victor Butt, Chief Engineer, is third from the left with the straw boater. Most of the rest are unknown.

Engine driver E. East had a pay increase in 1907 from 17/- to 23/-

'Dragon' broke 3 crankshafts during its lifetime. Victor Butt manufactured new crankshafts on the premises, making them stronger and more accurately balanced than the ones supplied by the original maker, and they also lasted longer.

'Dragon' was sold in 1913 for £100.

'Firefly' was sold for £65 in 1915.

'Togo', two trailers, and spares sold in 1916 to Mr. Cooper of Pinkneys Green for £165.

'Onward' and two trailers, with spare wheels and parts, (£800 and £95) sold to Avery and Sons of Wheatley.

'Forward' and two trailers sold for £355.

Brass plate with lots of screw holes thought to have been fitted to a steam engine.

'Progress' was the first lorry to be named and to be fitted with a brass name plate. The brass plates on the brewery lorries were to become very conspicuous over the next 80 years around the Marlow area. It was a chain driven Hallford with solid tyres and Acetylene lamps.

At the time it was a very basic, common truck bought in October 1911 for £649.10s. 0d. The addition of 'Progress' was deemed necessary, as the company had acquired 9 extra public houses as a result of the takeover of Bird's Brewery, Reading, 'Progress' was commandeered by the war department on 16th August 1914.

On October 10th 1913 it was valued in the accounts at £434.5s.10d.

Less depreciation £72.4s.4d.

£362.1s.6d net

Headboards advertising the brewery name first appeared in 1911.

This is usually what happened when the war department sent the lorries off to France…

Apologies for the quality, but this is a very rare picture and was thus considered to be worth including.

New 'Progress' the third Aveling, came with electric lighting for £41.13s.4d.

In 1914 they were using B.P petrol, storing some 5,000 gallons, at 1/3d a gallon in steel barrels.

Advance' suffered a cracked crankcase. There was a great deal of trouble with these crankcases, and after much wrangling with Aveling and Porter, they finally settled on supplying a new engine in 1919 for £245.

The brewery was very pleased with the new lorries as they were much faster, cleaner and only needed two men, whereas a traction engine needed three men and was useless in the snow - a big money saving all round.

All three Avelings were sold to Coxeter of Oxford minus the bodies for not less than £550.

The brewery looked after their employees. In 1902, the manager with instructions from the board, placed Walter Bowles, son of the late G Bowles, in a home for waifs and strays, and also obtained a promise that the elder brother would be admitted subject to a donation of £10 for the two boys,

There would also be a further expense of about £1 each for outfits and travelling expenses.

Driver, W. Chamberlain, received a donation of £20 to complete the cost of an outfit for his daughter to enable her to enter the institution for the blind.

'Always' - A very rare photo of an Aveling & Porter petrol lorry; they were better known for steam tractors.

It is seen here outside the works at Rochester, Kent, probably going on test since there appears to be wheels of a traction engine on the back. The author actually swapped a poster of a bullfight for this photo in a frame! The management are quoted as saying that, moving from steam to petrol, the men looked more like brewers' draymen than chimney sweeps! The author suggests they should have taken another look!

William Wiltshire's name appears over the door; he ran the Red Lion pub and agency at Chinnor.

The driver leaning on the radiator is G. Lefevre, who left in 1917 and rejoined in 1947 for a few months at the age of 64.

'Always' delivering to the Wheatsheaf in Slough about 1917. 'Always' was bought for £662 on December 17th 1913 – Reg. KT 886

The second Aveling to arrive was 'Advance' – Reg. D 9038

'Progress' was a third Aveling and Porter, bought later for £680 when the Hallford was taken by the war department.

'Always' had a Wethered sign and electric lights fitted in 1916 for £67.

A spare magneto was purchased for each lorry costing £20.

1913 - Probably the earliest Wethered Brewery lorry crash...

A MOTOR LO█████ SMASH. — On Wednesday, just before noon, a █████ motor lorry belonging to Thomas Wethered a████████ Ltd., of Great Marlow, turned into Market-█████ High-street. At that time a pony trap belo████ ██o Mr. Greville Palmer was standing on the left ██nd side of the road. To avoid a collision the driver turned to the right, the motor skidded, mounted the pavement, and crashed into the shop window of Mr. Clayton, hairdresser, breaking the window frame, displacing the iron standard supporting the building, and smashing the windows, parts of the motor entering the premises. The trap which the motor tried to avoid was badly damaged, but the pony was not hurt, and fortunately the vehicle was not occupied at the time of the collision.

'PERSEVERANCE' (PERCY) AND 'FORWARD'
THE FIRST THORNYCROFTS

'Perseverance' and 'Forward' were the first Thornycrofts to arrive in March 1919, Jack Lennard Snr. driving with mate Harry White.

THE LENNARD FAMILY ALL TOGETHER

Jack 'Gopot' *(far right)* and wife Lily. Victorine is in front of mum and sister May. Second left, father Garrett Lennard. Garrett, known as 'The Commodore', came from the Royal Marine Artillery. He knew nothing about horses, so he was taught to look after them and drive, he was also taught to drive steam lorries. Later came petrol lorries which he managed most successfully. On the declaration of war he was at once called up, and was soon promoted to sergeant. He was on the western front for four years and did excellent service.

'Victor', *pictured above,* a Thornycroft 2 ton BT Model. In 1921, as long as no overtime was incurred, 'Victor' served as a coach for the cricket and bowls teams to away matches. In 1930 the brewery equipped their 4 ton lorries with pneumatic tyres at a cost of £175. The changeover from solid to pneumatic was carried out by the brewery engineers.

Sir Walter Gilbey, Chairman of the London Cart Horse Parade Society, remarked at the 1925 London Parade, as he walked round with the then Home Secretary William Joynson Hicks those engines were so clean one could eat one's dinner off them.

In the 1920's this 2 ton trailer was purchased in conjunction with a lorry for £123.10s.0d
A similar trailer was commandeered by the War Department and hired to them for 7/6d per week.

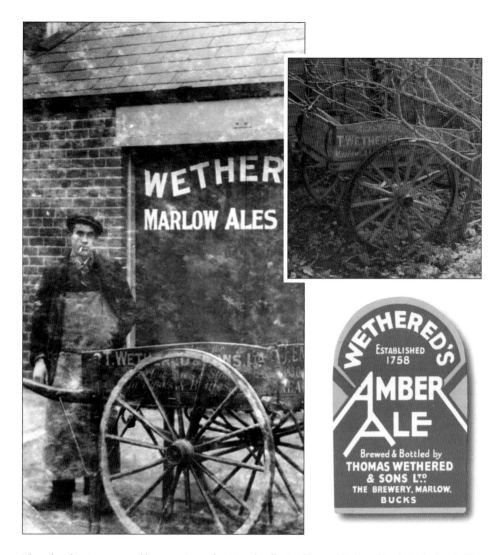

These handcarts were used by agencies such as Bracknell, Reading and Bidmead's of Maidenhead. The cost, new, in 1912 was £29.7s.6d.

The handcart top right is now languishing in someone's garden. The one above belonged to the Reading Agency and in 1911 it sold 1500 barrels whilst the Bracknell Agency sold 577 barrels.

The Railway arrived in Marlow in 1873, but it was not until 22 years later that the brewery began to use rail as a method of transport, starting in 1895. In 1900, drayman E Buckle, was employed solely to take the beer to the station by horse dray; he was paid an extra 1/- a week in addition to his ordinary wage to compensate him for loss of money on empties. Being the oldest drayman, and employed for 36 years, he was also used as watchman on Sundays between 4-9pm for an extra 1/6d.

Wines and spirits were also delivered in large barrels by rail and collected by brewery draymen.

The rail costs in 1903 totalled £3532.11s 2d.

On the 16th June 1913, rail was used to take employees on their outing to Weston-Super-Mare. The company paid for all tickets at a cost 5/- per head.

In 1973, the year of the Marlow Donkey Centenary Celebrations, there was a donation of 10 kegs of Whitbread Trophy bitter and free dispensing.

Centenary Booklet

1873   1973
100 Years Of The
MARLOW
DONKEY

Twenty Pence

'Victor' was a very smart A2 Thornycroft bought in October 1927. For most of her life she was driven by Cyril Simmonds. This was the first vehicle to arrive with pneumatic tyres.

Notice the bars fitted on the inside on the body to stop barrels buffeting the rails, which are set low for easier unloading.

'Vivid' was a very similar lorry, arriving in December 1929, at a cost of £405 and weighed 30 cwts. The rest of the fleet were mainly J types and the cost new, including lighting set and speedometer, was £855.

'Perseverance'	Reg. No:	HO 2298	March 1919
'Forward'		HO 2299	March 1919
'Onward'		HO 2348	June 1919
'Victor'		HO 2974	January 1920 2 Ton BT Model
'Always'		BH 6867	February 1920
'Progress'		HO 2975	December 1920
'Advance'		BH 0521	February 1921
'Powerful' type JJ		PP 9439	December 1927 cost £1051
'Peerless' type JJ		KX 1899	February 1929
A2 'Victor'		PP 9254	October 1927
A1 'Vivid'		unknown	December 1929

When 'Victor' was 7 years old in 1927, the chassis was sold back to Thornycroft for £75 and replaced with the latest W D chassis.

A 1930 picture showing the fleet in front of steam heated garages. These used to be open dray sheds and stables. In the far right corner was the hospital for sick horses, later it was the electrician's shop.

'Peerless', a Thornycroft JJ, was a 6 tonner bought in 1929 for £1095 to replace two 4 tonners. It was able to assist with the extra work involved from the takeover of William's Brewery, Wooburn. If the barrels were full then it would appear that the lorry is overloaded. Johnny Bond used to get inside the Strong Brown Ale advertising bottle and walk about with it

'Perseverance' returning to Thornycroft to go on show in their museum, this picture was taken at Thornycroft's yard, (not the brewery yard as noted in another publication!) It shows Garrett Lennard dropping off 'Percy' and picking up 'Always' as the replacement in 1946. As old lorries were replaced the brass name plates were removed and fitted to new lorries.

Thornycroft sent 'Perseverance' back to the brewery in 1969, after being taken over by Leyland and no longer being required. Before going out to many steam rallies she underwent a repaint in 1970 carried out by Chris Hope of Henley at a cost of £130. All painting was done by hand and the medals on the doors were gold leafed. *From the left:* John Hodgkinson, Bill Mudie, Head Brewer Bill Fisher, Tony Wilkinson and Jack Lennard, with his daughter Jenny.

Cyril Simmonds standing alongside 'Victor' in front of the mineral store. He retired in 1965 after 43 years service.

Charlie Clark leaning on 'Forward', he later moved into the transport office. Charlie was another 25 year man.

'Owen', a Bedford, one of two which came from Strange's Brewery, Aldermaston. *Left to right:* Bill Towers (Carpenter), Bill Clark, Norman Austin, and Frank Brooks.

A picture taken at the King's Head, Little Marlow, in the 1950's, the inn sign of Henry VIII being a cut-out instead of a pictorial hanging board. 'Beer is Best' is the slogan on the front of 'Perseverance', an advertising message that many brewers used at the time. In the cab, as you looked down you could see the road - an early form of air conditioning!

'Victor' being cleaned by Lawrie Langley, standing on a wooden crate – (probably not the health and safety officer)! On the left is driver, Harry Langley, (no relation).

Two real characters ...
Ron Carter with a pint and Alf 'Monty' Webb wearing his beret, Ron later went on to work at Marlow Post Office.

The sign below is for Monty, it was a well known fact that he took two days getting back from Romsey Brewery.

This sign was fitted to the rear of the Sturdys and Seddons.

Basil Poulton, a 52 year service man leaning on 'Owen'. In the background is Dick 'Tiger' Cooper.

Stan Turner could get an extra pint out of any landlord, just by telling him it's the best one he's had all day. "Any chance of another, governor?", and, yes, he did like a pint or two. When he was younger he used to box in the yard at the back of the Clayton Arms.

Eric Rollings: No he's not a window cleaner; he's using the ladder to check the loads on the trailers.

Left, Dick 'Tiger' Cooper, Wally Griffin, unknown and Ron Carter understood to be on an outing.

Alan Sykes 'just call me Sykes' with his famous sleeveless jumper. He was only ever seen once with a sleeved jumper and when told he was caught out, his reply was, "No you're wrong I've got it on underneath!" Alan is seen here delivering to the Bull at Sonning.

'Owen' and 'Fortis' name plates were introduced in 1959, the 'Stanley' name plate cost £1.2s.4d in 1960. The last Seddon sold was 'Peerless' driven by Basil Tegg 1972.

The fleet of Seddons: Photo taken by the Pound Lane gates. When purchased new the price depended on which engine was fitted. A Perkins engine & auto mechanical lubrication was £2121.14s.0d. An AEC engine & mechanical lubrication was £2441.17s.0d. Some were also fitted with Leyland engines. The photo below was taken at the King's Head, Little Marlow.

This picture has often been published before, but you might be unaware of the reason for this line-up. These were the drivers that won an award (below) for going a year without any accidents; if that was all it took to get the award it doesn't say much for the other drivers! From *left to right:* Harry Langley, Ollie Hodges, Frank 'Topper' Wye, Jim Thorne, Dick 'Tiger' Cooper, Andy Farrell, Stan Turner, Henry Pilgrim, and plumber, David Baker.

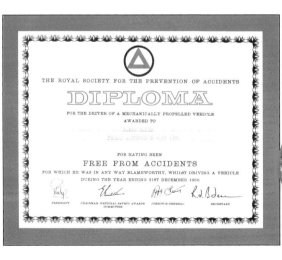

The Green Ford before being sprayed Whitbread Brown. The name 'Freddie' first appeared on a Ford in 1969 being named after the Head Brewer at Romsey – Freddie Toogood.

Jan in 'Perseverance', a brown Ford in Whitbread livery. In the early days they were prone to blowing head gaskets. Having got over that problem, they were forever breaking rear springs, probably due to overloading. The body was made by Marlow Coach Works in Newtown Road, Marlow.

'Forward', a Ford D800 – there were two of these and two D300 3 Tonners, the rest were six wheel D500's. As the 500's got older, and, having been all bought together, a lot of the engines were blowing up at the same time. Around the yard it looked like a Ford graveyard!

One Saturday a group of draymen went to Sheffield to pick up three Dennis lorries below, but only two made it back as the rear wheel bearing of the third had collapsed. The author had to pick up the repaired Dennis from Northampton the following week; consequently these Dennis lorries didn't last very long either.

Driver's mate Eddie Walker and driver Bob Phassey.

A twin steer Bedford Chinese Six. She was a little odd to drive as both front axles steered. She arrived with a green transfer on the head-board, but obviously someone did not like the green headboards, so it was not long before they were changed to red.

'Amber' is above and 'Titan' is right. Their names first appeared when the Reading depot closed, and everything moved across to Marlow.

Whitbread were one of the first companies to have curtain sided lorries, far quicker for loading and unloading.

Photo taken in 1987, shows a Dodge which had just arrived, as odd ones sometimes did, depend-ing on what was going spare at other depots.

Ford 4 wheeler with solid rubber rear suspension, it just bounced along the road. They all came in this livery which later changed to the one below. Some were sprayed at a British Airways garage, and some at a garage in Thame. The cost was covered by the Whitbread Marketing Department.

2010 was not the only winter with bad snow: here is 'Onward' going absolutely nowhere. Clearing the snow was a regular additional task in severe winters. Dave Crosk is on the forklift truck. The author can remember picking the snow plough up from Swindon 30 years ago.

An advert from the 1950's

Left, 'Perseverance' with 'Wethered' on the right, what a difference seventy years can make. A 1919 Thornycroft carrying 4 tons and on the right, a 1991 Ford Cargo that could carry three times as much. The new Ford was just part of a £750,000 programme to change the fleet. The King's Head at Little Marlow was a popular location to take photographs.

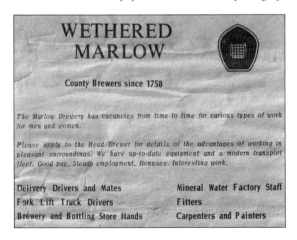

A 1963 advert from the Bucks Free Press: Plenty of vacancies if you were looking for a job, in the 1970's it was an advantage if you played football. In the 80's it helped if you knew someone who already worked at the brewery. Up until the mid sixties there was a vacancy board which hung on the outside of the White House.

'Victor'

Just a few of many accidents, most occurred on the road but there were quite a few in the yard as well.

'Strong'

'Freddie'

Phil Lewington, looking very proud. He's just dropped his Chinese Six over the side terracing at Marlow Football Club's Alfred Davis ground.

A new generation Ford, which was longer, lower and had an area for an extra working pallet. It was much easier for loading and unloading and less stress on the draymen's backs. Seen here is Melvyn Deri, assistant transport manager overseeing the loading.

Two Fords with two different liveries

'Always' with a broken near side step, which was a common fault.

'Freddie' before the crash.

Draymen lined up in the top yard on their last day, from left: Paul 'Hon Sec' Burdell, Frank Steptoe, Karl Budd, Steve Probert, Alan Stevens, Chris Flint, Trevor Painter, Pete 'Ginger' Hawes, John Brainch, Ron Swadling, Pete Hogan and Mick Hart.

More draymen and warehouse staff just kicking their heels and drinking their last cups of coffee; a few names: Ken Coker, Trevor 'Jumbo' Howard, Pete Hickman, Mick 'Spud' Taylor, the back of Keith Budd, Andy Weldon.

The last dray to leave the yard; draymen Brian 'Buller' Bowles and Nigel North giving a final salute on April 23 1993.

Farewell … 235 years wiped out with a stroke of a pen.

A real character here in drayman Basil Tegg, now aged 96 and still going strong. He was a driver in the Royal Army Service Corp during World War Two, he was captured in Greece and spent four years in Stalag xviii-a, a POW camp at Wolfsberg, Austria.

When working at the brewery he lived at Woodlands Park Maidenhead, some five miles from the brewery. He would ride his bicycle to work, very rarely having a day off.

Going home however was a different matter as there were a few pubs to be negotiated. Namely the Golden Ball, Robin Hood, Wagon and Horses and the New Inn – he would sink a few pints and then arrive home about 10 pm to meet his long suffering wife affectionately known as 'the old pullet'.

Prior to working at Wethered's he worked at 'Nicks' – Nicholson's Brewery Maidenhead – which was taken over by Courage in 1959.

Jack Edwards fancying himself as a jockey, this lion thought to be taken down from above the entrance to the Red Lion, High Wycombe. His father *right,* John Edwards, was in the winning lorry team. There were many employees from the same family – for example at one time, in the early years there were the Swadlings, in later years there were 4 Bowles, 4 Norths, 3 Taylors and not forgetting the Lennards: Garrett, his son Jack, and Jack's twin daughters Jenny and Jacqui.

Back Row: A.J.West, W.O.Swadling, R.Boddy.
Front Row: Joe Tubb, Harry White, Garrett Lennard, Victor Butt, J.Edwards.

When Wethered's purchased their first J Type 4-ton lorries from Thornycroft in Basingstoke in 1919, little did they realise they would not only be used to deliver beer, but the meticulous care afforded by their drivers would result in the company winning awards and prestige in various national competitions.

As soon as the lorries had been delivered to each drayman, they ensured that their machine would be kept in immaculate condition even to the extent of voluntarily staying on after work to polish and clean every part of the vehicle including the engine.

Three vehicles arrived in that first year, 'Perseverence' and 'Forward' in March, and 'Onward' in June, each costing £855. Their wonderful brass nameplates, in the same way as those of GWR steam locomotives, gave each lorry that individual identity which guaranteed a gasp of admiration as they drove through the town and local villages. Two more vehicles were added to the fleet in 1920, 'Always' in February followed by 'Progress' in December, whilst 'Victor' and 'Advance' were to follow soon after.

Proud of their wonderful delivery vehicles it was the drivers who decided in 1921 to enter a team in the parade organised by the Reading Comrades and Veteran's Association. Before setting off for the competition, the three Thornycroft vehicles selected were 'Perseverance', 'Onward' and 'Forward', attended by each driver and mate. The Chief Engineer Mr. V.B. Butt and the Managing Director Colonel F.E. Stevens would inspect the vehicles and congratulate the draymen on the condition of the lorries. They were then applauded by staff and visitors as they set off for Reading.

They were so successful that they lifted the C.M.U.A. silver trophy and again in 1922. However, the organisers in Berkshire hated the publicity Wethered's (from Bucks), were receiving so they retaliated by restricting entry to a 10 mile radius of Reading Town Hall. This petty bureaucracy did not bother these proud men of Marlow, as they had in 1922, already won the Commercial Motor Challenge Cup in London, a far more prestigious national competition.

An impressive line up at Lincoln's Inn Fields, London. This major national annual event which had been inaugurated in 1910 had a long list of winning companies who were household names, with Shell Mex Ltd. being the current holders. Thomas Wethered took this competition by storm entering the same three Thornycroft lorries, 'Perseverance', 'Onward' and 'Forward' which had been so successful in Reading.

Winning this competition not only gave the brewery fantastic publicity it also gave the drivers and their mates celebrity status in Marlow.

The meticulous care afforded to their lorries resulted in them not only winning the cup in 1922, but they repeated this achievement again in 1923 and 1924, resulting in them being awarded the cup outright. They voluntarily withdrew from the competition but the organisers asked them to be on show for the next three years which they willingly did.

Two teams entered, the winning team drivers were G.J. Lennard, J. Tubb, and C.H. White, the second team 'Progress', 'Advance' and 'Always', the drivers being Edwards, West and Boddy. They were highly commended in 1922, second in 1923, and fifth in 1924.

25 March 1922 expenses incurred attending the parade
Food and lodgings for men and garage … … … … … … … … … … … …£5.15s 4 ½d
Prize money to drivers £1 and mates 10/- … … … … … … … … … … … £10. 0s 0d
Petrol 66 gallons @ 1s 10.1/2d … … … … … … … … … … … … … … £ 6. 3s 9d
Total - …£ 21.19s 1½d

Presenting the cups are, from left, Victor Butt, Mr. Shrapnell Smith and Colonel F. E. Stevens.

A cask washing shed packed with brewery workers, their wives and children; the presentation of trophies was a major event in the history of the brewery.

It's inspection time, with Colonel Stevens seen walking away, the Colonel always took a special interest in the transport. On his appointment, the firm had 52 horses. By the time motor transport was fully introduced, there were only three horses remaining. On the left is W.O. Swadling with Alf West looking on.

Plenty of happenings around the cask shed! Here are the drivers and mates receiving their trophies. Seated are V. Butt (left) and Col. Stevens (right), rear, behind the table is Mr. Shrapnell Smith, with drivers, left, Tubb, Swadling, Boddy, Lennard, and right, White, Edwards, and West.

In 1903, Victor Bertram Butt, whilst employed by Crompton and Co. of Chelmsford, supervised the installation of electric power at the brewery. Soon after, Colonel Stevens offered him the post of head electrician as Mr Parsons had been dismissed for being drunk whilst on duty. In 1907, Victor Butt was made Chief Engineer.

Butt was instrumental in bringing steam engines to the brewery and had his wages increased to 50/- a week in consideration of the extra work entailed by locomotives during 1905.

1907: Butt was living at "Kinclaven", Little Marlow Road when his wages were increased to £156 per annum with the board's approval.

1908: They gave him a bonus in consideration of outside engineering work that he had carried out for the company; another bonus was to come in 1912 of £15 plus a wage increase to £190.

1913: Carelessness by a bricklayer's labourer allowed a bucket of lime to fall on Mr. Butt's suit and he was paid £2.2s.0d. so he could have it cleaned.

1921: Allan & Simmond's, an engineering firm of Reading, offered Butt the post of Works Manager at a salary of £450 per annum, in view of his excellent reputation and his qualifications as an electrician and mechanical motor engineer. It was resolved to increase his salary to £500 per annum in order to retain his services.

1921: 'Perseverance' won first prize in the 30 Guineas Cup at Reading on a bank holiday. J. Lennard won a teapot which the company bought from him and then presented to Mr. Butt in 1921. They also purchased an oak cabinet from driver Lennard for £3.3s.0d who had won it at the Reading competition and this was also given to Butt.

1922: The engineer's prize was awarded to Butt for showing best condition at the London Commercial Motor Challenge Cup. £1 was awarded to drivers and 10/- to mates once again.

Butt had a slight malformation of one big toe; it was not a serious condition until a shell bar fell on it, as at the time the brewery was involved in making munitions. The company paid £48.5s.3d for treatment and an operation, this was in 1923.

It was often left to Butt to thank the company for organising the outings.

Butt retired on 31 July 1947 after 43 years service, and requested the lorry cup be given to him.

Victor Bertram Butt was a brilliant engineer, there was very little he could not do, but he also knew when to ask for a wage increase. He died in 1951.

He was also a past master of Marlow Lodge of Freemasons; he had been to a meeting the night before he was found dead in bed at the George and Dragon, Marlow.

Still winning cups 54 years later with the same lorry. 1978: The London to Brighton Commercial Vehicle Rally, held every year on the first Sunday in May. The author, left, and Kelvin Gryckiewicz, receiving three cups from Lord Montague of Beaulieu.

1st Surrey Cup - best in class (over 3 tons).

1st Montague Cup - best up to year 1920.

1st Leyland trophy - best truck or fire engine in the entire rally.

The rally usually consists of about 200 vintage vehicles starting at Battersea Park, then on to Brighton. It's not a race, judging takes place once vehicles are parked on the sea front. There were two brewery Thornycrofts in this rally. The other drivers were Jan Hoare, Wally Griffin, Stan Flint and Frank Steptoe, plus two coach loads of brewery employees supporting Wethereds.

Two more cups from the Holyport Show, the author on the left and his son Matthew on the right.

Winning cups for fuel trials are, from the left, Mick Mitchell, Alec 'Jock' Milne, Brian Webb and Keith Budd. Known as the Gordon Goddard Fuel Economy Trials, this was a fairly new competition starting in 1981, named after a late Whitbread engineer and held at the Mira test track, Nuneaton. The idea was to go round the track at a set speed to see who would use the least fuel.

Alec Milne and Brian Webb were the drivers with Mick Mitchell acting as an observer. A small detachable tank was fitted behind the cab containing a set amount of fuel.

The first year this team entered, they won 11 awards plus best overall entry of 7.45 m.p.g., they also won in the following 2 years making 3 in succession, and all with the same 38 ton lorry ERF – Reg. No. B352 KAN 'Powerful'.

Brian aged 13 in the Marlow Town Band.

Foreman Fred Simmonds, *left,* George Keeley, *centre,* who started in 1950 straight from school and left in 1953 to join the army. Stan Beaver, *right,* a painter who painted the lorries and the pubs, the lorry above being a Commer. The boilerhouse and oil tanks can be seen in the background.

The garage was moved at least three times. It started in the building which is visible behind the employees in the munitions photo then moved up into the top yard in what were the old stables. It moved again in 1972 to the beer store off Pound Lane.

Wages in 1919 per week …

F Nicholls Snr.. .... 70/-
T Golding, fitters assistant 50/-
A Coventry, fitters assistant ... 50/-
F Nicholls, junior boy 36/-
F J Simmons 34/-
J Harvey 34/-
F Newman 25/-

Some of the very first engineers: Newman, Harvey & Coventry

Harold Fletcher

Peter Harding, electrician *(left)* and Bill Stroud electrician's mate, photo taken in about 1958. Peter's predecessor was Harold Fletcher, *above,* who left and became a well known Marlow photographer; maybe that is why there were a lot of photos taken around that time. Bill was in the lorry winning team in the 1920's

Fred Simmonds, garage foreman from the 50's to the mid 70s.

His father Vic, *above,* cleaning the car was a chauffeur at the brewery.

Stan Ridge was another employee who came from Strong's of Romsey. He oversaw the building of the new offices and warehouse, and was also in charge of the building department. Carpenters, plumbers, painters and a gang of builders from Aldermaston were responsible for the up keep of approx 250 pubs.

Carpenters' workshop

Question - could anyone work in a mess like this? Answer –Yes! Workshop foreman John Harris.

The building of the new warehouse; it was built by the brewery building department, and the steel work erected by Condors of Winchester. *Above:* Harry 'Concert' James, second right, Albert Webb and the Aldermaston gang, their wages would have been £19 1s 8d.

The front office girls *(right)* attending the opening of the new warehouse and office in 1973.

Harry, *bottom,* still leaning on his shovel, working on the new offices next to the warehouse. His favourite saying was, "what I'm going to do today wouldn't hurt anybody."

Signwriter Ken Mansfield painting the Old Sun at Lane End. Notice the Wethered writing on the gable ends – it is still there today, even though the pub has recently closed.

Ken at work on a pictorial in his workshop. He was one of the last brewery signwriters. A fairly simple design could take about 18 hours to complete.

When the signs came in they had to be stripped right back after being damaged by the elements and children with air guns!

Ken's favourite sign was the Falcon at Denham which featured a Peregrine Falcon. He says "it's the most pleasing piece of work I've ever done".

Kelvin Gryckiewicz, *above,* Home Counties bantam weight boxing champion, worked in the garage 1975 – 78.

The author, *right,* jacking the front axle up on 'Powerful' in order to adjust the brakes.

Mick Mitchell, foreman. 1975 - 1993.

GUILTY!

On one rather icy morning, Frank Steptoe was reversing a trailer down the ramp into the garage for a service. The trailer slipped on the ice-covered ramp and hit the pier with devastating effects.

Seeing it pulled away shortly afterwards, camera in hand, the author said to Dave, "one brick should do the trick." The result is seen below.

This is the workshop just off Pound Lane or rather it was!

Rob Westall, *(left)*, worked on fire engines before starting at the brewery. Unfortunately, he started not long before the brewery closed.

Ernie Foster, *(right)*, fork lift truck fitter.

Dave Crosk, *(left)*, repairing a radiator. There is a Britvic lorry in the background on the lift being repaired under outside contract.

A Boulton and Watt boiler of 1836 working at 5lbs per sq. inch gave power to water and wort pumps. The malt mill hoist and yeast press would have been belt driven as in the photo below. Pulleys were widespread throughout the brewery and bottlery.

The boiler is always referred to as 'the engine'. Before the installation of the James Watt, horse power was used with the horses using a circular track gearing.

On other occasions man power was employed, in later years this unit served as a hot liquor tank, liquor being the brewer's term for water.

The front of the boiler, *above,* can still be seen, just off Pound Lane.

The photo below was taken in what is now the Pound Lane car park, with a view across to the two brewery chimneys. It depicts a fleet of Tillion's lorries, a carriage firm with a yard and offices in Dean Street. The smaller chimney is for the James Watt boiler.

A 1970's photo, *(top left)*, showing the base of this chimney with trees growing out of it. The 'Lest We Forget' shovel was last used in 1968.

The last days of the coal fired Galloway boilers. In the above photo are engineer Jan Hoare and stokers Bill Davis & Wally Griffin. These two boilers were only used for one month while the oil fired Lancashire boilers had their annual overhaul.

Left, Porter's modern transport!

On the 1st of January 1900, an employee of Porter's was returning some wooden barrels, rolling them by the cask shed area and unfortunately broke the leg of a cask washer worker, Fred Grace.

Porter's of Marlow was one of the main suppliers of coal along with companies like Dunlop's of Reading plus Cory's of London and Birmingham. Porter's tender was accepted for supplying the following….

Wyken Hand Ryder steam coal at 18/9 per ton.

Household coal from Cannock Chase 22/- per ton.

Smith's coal from Hollybush colliery 23/3 per ton.

The brewery would keep 9 weeks' coal in stock.

Edwin Hall joined the company in 1868; he spent 6 years in the yard, and then became head stoker. In 1904 he started day and night shifts, but was unable to keep awake. As a result he was taken off night work and put on to the day shift as requested by the brewer. To make life easier he was transferred to the cask shed as the boiler there was just for the cask washer.

It was reported that he was an indifferent stoker, who could not get about easily in order to oil machinery in the brewery. He eventually served 46 years. It was only discovered three years ago that Edwin was the author's great grandfather.

Edwin Hall's wages: 14/- per week in 1870

14/- per week in1888 – no increase 18 years on!

His wages went up to 20/- per week (£1) for 4 weeks during the harvest period, 24th August to 14th September, since Wethered's were farmers as well as brewers.

Here are some notable events from past years:

James Swadling was instantly dismissed for being drunk and letting his boiler go out.

William Hillsden was sacked for being drunk in charge of a boiler which would probably have exploded - 7th January 1905.

Letting the boiler go out, or letting it run low on water, resulted in major problems and usually meant not starting it up again until the following lunch time. Loss of production was the obvious consequence.

In June 1903 Lovells built the new boiler house and engine & battery room for £249.4s.0d.

New lightning conductor fitted on new chimney for £13.0s.0d

The two package boilers pictured below, are a Lincoln and a Cradley. The Cradley on the right arrived in July 1982, the Lincoln arrived in August 1986, only to be used for 2 years before being taken out again. And here is someone else who cannot seem to keep awake, and this was in the daytime! All he has to do is watch the gauge! It is Derek Painter! At least Edwin used a shovel.

The original brewery office built in 1808 is seen here with the Bell Tower. It was used later as the wine and spirit store. It had to move to the top yard in the blacksmith's shop in 1929, in order to enable the bottling plant to expand as demand grew. The bell was used to inform workers of starting and finishing times. A new bell (which can still be seen) was fitted in 1901 but was replaced by a steam hooter in 1914, however there were instructions that this must not be sounded at 6am. The area underneath is now a car park for the new offices.

The photo below, shows the loading stage erected in 1907 for £38, and the overhead 2½" copper pipes that carry the beer from the brewhouse to the bottling hall, pipes fitted by brewery specialists Worssam for £92.00 in1909.

Some doubts about exactly what bottles Fred, Pat and Nellie are filling, but it may be one of the labels pictured below, and possibly ginger wine. A 45 year old bottle of this still tastes marvellous!

Purchased a corking machine in January 1907 for £8 10s 0d.

A new still was put in at a cost of £16 13s 4d in 1917

1919 purchased 6 Hogsheads of brandy over 3 years at 34/- a gallon.

Seen above are Fred Tubb, Pat Burnham and Brian North. Wine and spirits were delivered in Hogsheads. The casks of wine, pipes of port and butts of sherry were received by rail, picked up by our men and let down the cellars, then on to the racks where the barrels stand, which is known as a stillage. After fining, they were left for ten days before tapping and bottling.

At this time wine and spirits were sold by the Jar (1/2 gallon 1 gallon and 2 gallon).

Spirit order, 5 Hogsheads of Glen Grant Whisky in 1917 - 25/- a gallon

20 Hogsheads '8 years Old' Whisky - 27/-

4 Hogsheads 'Irish Old' Whiskey - 30/-

Nellie Rogers, *left,* seen filling the wine rack. Wines were re-introduced in 1928 after being discontinued for some years.

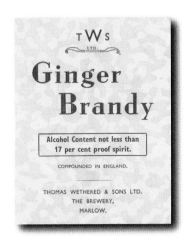

Nellie Rogers with Madeline Rogers, no relation.

Wethered's bought a bicycle in 1907 for £5.10s.0d. This is not it, but it was undoubtedly similar!

Herbert 'Herbie' Swadling, was born above the Crown Hotel in 1890, he started at the Brewery on 10/- a week, in 1907. By 1909 he was in charge and earning £1 a week. He, like Fred and Brian below, served 50 years. Herbie was also president of Marlow Football Club.

150 YEARS SERVICE BETWEEN THE THREE OF THEM

Brian North, Fred Tubb and Herbie at Fred's 50 year presentation, held at the George and Dragon Hotel. Fred started work on his 14th birthday in January 1930. His father also worked as a stoker at the brewery. He started as a boy gardener and then delivered minerals by horse and cart. In 1936 he went into the wine and spirit store.

Brian North, *(centre)*, at a presentation in the Cavern Club to mark his 50 years with the company. Joe Walker, Managing Director, *(right)*, and transport manager Dave Wotton, *(left)*.

Brian is seen filling bottles which were corked at that time. The corking machine was bought in 1907 for £8.10s.0d.

The Cellar Service Department, just off the High Street, where you will now find the Slug and Lettuce. It was built by Lovells for £563 in 1879, originally housing the Wethered family's stables and horse driven carriage.

This photo shows the brickwork which is just to the left of the black door in the top photo and shows the family's initials. When the building was pulled down the bricks were taken to Remnantz, the Wethered family home in West Street.

Cellar Service is a department in the brewery which specialises in installing and servicing dispensing equipment in bars and cellars of public houses and clubs.

John 'Snowy' Austin, *(left)*, with Jim Brainch, *(on the right)*; two cellar service storemen who also refurbished beer coolers

June 1973, Brian Boulton and Peter Butler on a 'jolly' at the Post House Hotel enjoying free beer tasting, just two of the keg fitters that came over from the Reading depot when it closed. The pyramid of Party Kings 4 pint cans long since gone.

Drayman Jim Greig, taking instructions from cellar service boss Mike Holliday who designed and built the trailer affectionately known as 'Mr Cow' and used for outside functions. Cellar service fitter Bob Thomas is seen dragging out the lengths of beer hoses; there were lots of people dragging mobile bars around to shows, but very few had a mobile cellar.
Inset: Mike Holliday.

Above, a Land Rover and mobile bar which came from Romsey in the late 1960's. Later the Land Rover was painted yellow and used by the garage for recovery.

138

Most of the Cellar Service staff shown above left, set up for a training session for the landlords, and in the photo on the right note 'Ivor Goodpint'; some of the landlords needed the training as the author has had quite a few bad pints!

Another father and son, this time working in cellar service, Sid Prince *on the left* and his son Gary. Sid started by working for a contractor delivering beer and was then successful when applying for a permanent job on the drays. Due to problems with his back, as happened with many draymen, Sid moved across to cellar service. Gary having seen so many changes after 26 years, left and recently started with Marlow's micro brewery Rebellion.

In the mid 1960's there were just three cellar service staff but by the early 1990's the number had risen to 20.

Ted Drake top English footballer, came to Wethered's when Whitbread closed the Reading depot.

Ted started his career at Southampton, having being born there, but made his name at Arsenal where he won two League titles and an FA Cup. He holds the record for most goals scored in a game in the top league in England, scoring seven for Arsenal against Aston Villa in December 1935. He also played for England five times.

When his career ended he went on to manage Reading and Chelsea. A real all-rounder, as he also played cricket for Hampshire.

The 1984 wine education trip to Calvet France, taking time off for a kick about on a racecourse, unfortunately, John Erbes injured his foot in a horse divot. One of the reps, Mark Derry, left shortly afterwards and founded the Loch Fyne chain of restaurants with Ian Glyn, then sold out to Greene King Brewery in 2007 for £68m, and took over the Brasserie Blanc chain of restaurants from Raymond Blanc.

Back row: Mike Hocking, Adam Holmes, John Erbes, Jeff Carter, Jean Tompkins, Mike Wrigley, Mike Holliday, Peter Harwood, Mark Derry, Francis Golding.

Front row: Dennis Woods, Bryan Humphrey, Mark Watson, Tony Walton, Barry Hunt, Eric Martin, Nick Price and Tony Wilkinson.

An annual event for the reps was to make their own Christmas cards, and off to Jolliffe's fancy dress shop in Marlow. This photo shoot was taken at the Hinds Head in Bray, Berkshire, which is now owned by renowned chef Heston Blumenthal. Most of the names: Nick Price, Mark Watson, Jeff Carter, John Erbes, Bob Anderson, Tony Wilkinson, Tony Walton, Mike Hocking, Sandra Hyde, Bryan Humphrey as Father Xmas, David Pratt, and Eric Martin.

A greetings card that was given to visitors at reception.

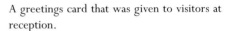

Two more cards that were generally given out

This photo was taken in the back room of the Cavern Club. *Left to right:* Barry Hunt, Diane Cusden, Tony Wilkinson, Sandra Hyde, Jill Reagan, Peter Harwood, Mark Watson, Mike Wrigley, Bob Anderson, Eric Martin, John Erbes, Bryan Humphrey, Tony Walton, Adam Holmes, Nick Price, Mike Hocking.

"O Sing Choirs of Angels"

Two photos taken in Marlow Church. *From the top:* Tony Wilkinson, Simon Cartwright, Paul Reid, Mike Hocking, Francis Golding, Ray Iliff, Adam Holmes, Barry Stamford, Colin Rogan. *Front, from the left:* Eric Martin, Tony Walton, Sandra Hyde, Jonathon Glenny, Sharon Dimbleby, Jane Roberts, Adam Jones; don't think I've missed anyone.

Opening of Bird Hills Golf Club, Maidenhead. The picture shows rep Mike Hocking *(far right)* with Tony Wilkinson, Free Trade Manager next to him. *Far left* is Clive Smith, designer of the golf club, Clive also owns racehorse Kauto Star, winner of two Cheltenham Gold Cups and four King George chases. Officially opening the golf club was Dennis Thatcher who was first to tee off.

Picture above was taken outside Theatre Royal, Windsor with the vintage vehicles in the background. Tony Wilkinson, far left, with actors, William Franklyn ("Schhh…You Know Who"), unknown, Stacy Dorning, star of 'Black Beauty' and Trevor Bannister (Dick James Lucas in 'Are You Being Served'). Gentleman at the back is Theatre Manager Mark Piper who is married to 'Marlene' from popular comedy 'Only Fools and Horses'. Tony seemed to have the best job in the brewery!

It didn't take much for the reps to jump on a jolly to Jerez, Spain to sample the delights of Domecq tipples. On the *far left* is Eric Martin, and the names of the other reps are: Norman Burrell, Joe Saunders, John Erbes, Francis Golding, Mike Wrigley, Barry Hunt, Jeff Carter, Keith Legg, Graham Liggins, Peter Harwood, Steve Middleton, Steve Chamberlain and Tony Wilkinson. The reps on the left crossing walking sticks had all been injured playing football. The people to the right of this picture are Domecq employees.

Hospitality in the evening from Domecq, picture showing Tony Wilkinson receiving a bottle from an employee known as 'the nose' for his expertise in blending sherry.

Yes you're right; it's me, the author, having taken 'Perseverance' to the opening of a new pub, the Monkey Puzzle Tree at Cove, Farnborough. Converted from a farm, after a few successful years the landlord sold it on to Whitbread, who now run it as a Brewer's Fayre, the reps stitched me up saying I was the only one the outfit would fit!

Dennis Gillett was manager of the off-licence for many years, and is seen here with his wife Beryl, who came to help him in 1969 for 3 weeks but stayed for 15½ years until closure in 1985. Dennis started in 1964, and in 1967 formed the brewery football team and became the manager. The team played in the Maidenhead & Slough District League.

Dennis and Beryl on the last day.

Dennis also had a licence for an outside bar, this picture was taken at an event re-enacting a civil war battle. *From the left:* Asa Biggs, Paul Templeman, Stan Flint, Dennis' son Adrian, Dennis' wife Beryl, Jan Smart, Dennis, unknown, unknown and John Keith.

Serving wenches, *from left,* Linda Swadling, Jill Collins, Lesley Payne and Shirley ? at Hambleden Fayre.

WETHERED NEWS

Thomas Wethered & Sons Ltd · The Brewery · Marlow

PILOT EDITION

SEPTEMBER 1977

THIS IS IT –
YOUR OWN NEWSPAPER !!

We ask the question – 'Do we need our own monthly news-medium?' – The only way we can find out is to 'Have a go' and ask for your opinion.

We think such a paper should be both informative and amusing, and at the same time be a platform for airing views – particularly with regard to our SOCIAL CLUB. We envisage – a Cavern Calendar – a Live Letter Column – News of pensioners – Introduction to new Starters and A Farewell to Leavers Column – Company History and News – Sports Fixtures and results – and in this copy, the PILOT EDITION, we have attempted to give a general 'mix' to whet the appetite.

We hope you enjoy it, and we [...] you to pass on any information or ideas for our next issue.

Thank You.

" THE EDITORS "

Wanted – a name !

Can you think up an apt name for this newspaper - at present called Wethered News - a HANDSOME PRIZE is on offer for the best idea....

Suggestions to Dave Lee....

INTRODUCTION FROM THE MANAGING DIRECTOR:

I am pleased to be able to write an introduction to the Wethered News – a new venture to which I wish every success. I believe that it is important that we try to improve our system of communication and one way of doing this is to produce a newspaper which tells everybody what is happening to people in other

NO. 13
OCTOBER 1978

WETHERED WORLD

Thomas Wethered & Sons Ltd · The Brewery · Marlow

3RD ANNUAL DARTS CHAMPIONSHIPS

Surprise followed surprise in the first rounds of the 3rd Annual Darts Championships played off in the Cavern last week. First being the early defeat of favourite Phil Lewington. Terry Ashby, of Stock Control, knocked out Peter Sparks, one time Whitbread London Cup-holder; Andrew Denton, newcomer in Vehicle Fitting finished Melvyn Deri's interest in the game, but brother Stewart Deri made the magic 'Triple 60' qualifying him for the Whitbread "180 Club".

'Mick' Wakefield did it the easy way with two walk-overs into the third round, but wife Angela did'nt survive the first round in the Ladies section in which the favourites fared much better. Ann Rowles – Lesley McNicol – Lynda Swadling and Carole Franklin are left to fight to a finish.
Every competitor was issued with a Draw ticket for a TREGNUM of WHISKY – to be presented on FINALS NIGHT – the winner must be present on the night.

Jointly edited with David Lee, this was originally the idea of Stan Wilson, to bring out a monthly newsletter. It would contain information such as starters/leavers and success in sports competitions. This first edition requested suggestions to name the newsletter, and resulted in *Wethered World* being selected.

A regular feature of 'Wethered World' was "Ray the Dray" and 'Personality of the Month'. As can be seen, Stan was a very good artist.

'WETHERED WORLD'

This is our first edition under our new title, and the winner of our NAMING COMPETITION was Cliff Budd in Load Planning Dept. His prize will be presented in the Cavern on Saturday evening 11th. February, together with Darts Presentation of awards.

WETHERED WORLD
Nº 10 JULY 1978

Thomas Wethered & Sons Ltd·The Brewery·Marlow

'LOVELY' CRICKET

There is much to be said for the 'mixed' game as a spectacle, and when the Ladies beat the Gentlemen as they did on 21st June that is a bonus. The star attraction was obviously Denise of Managed Houses who carried her bat for a superb 30 runs. This despite being hit on the leg and finding an overwhelming number of offers to provide massage treatment to the offended limb. The game was played on one of our colder, drizzly days on Marlow Sports Ground. It turns out that Denise spent some of her formative years in Ilkley, Yorks, nobbut more than a Draymans length from the birthplace of Hutton, Illingworth and Boycott - and there was a famous Yorkshire'all-rounder' called Roy Kilner in the 30's - any connection Denise ?

LEG BEFORE !

JACK COOK -RARE BIRD IN MANAGED HOUSE DEPARTMENT

Our Managed Houses Department found that they had one more bird than usual - one of the feathered variety this time. A starling paid a visit down the office chimney and Wendy Eastwell was a little perturbed to find a beak sticking through the grille behind her chair. No volunteer was keen to release the prisoner until wily old bird Jack arrived - he has a way with birds.

Welcome

Gregory (Greg) Barrett joined the company as Apprentice in Painting and Decorating on Tuesday 17th April. Greg whose father Tom is also with the Company (past Chairman of the Cavern Club) is a member of Marlow Boxing Club and is already asking if we have a Boxing Section - Anyone interested?

David Vance is welcomed to Cavern Club membership. David started in the Painting and Decorating Dept, in January but the fact was missed from the last edition of WW. Sorry David - but welcome nevertheless!

Moving on...

Denise Kilner of Managed House Department left the company to join Maritz of Marlow on 20th October.

Adrian Ford of Storage & Handling left the Company during October.

Moving In

Eileen McMillan joined the company on 25th October, to work in Computer Liaison.

RAY the DRAY..

THIS STUFF IS ALL CLOUDY

WHAT D YOU EXPECT FOR THE PRICE? THUNDER AND LIGHTNING!

ANNUAL CRICKET EVENT

The weather smiled once again on our annual Cricket match between Tenants & Managers versus the Brewery XI on Wednesday 27th. June

The visitors were a bit short on numbers when the game started at Marlow ground and rumour has it that they scored 60 or so, which was easily matched by the Brewery team spearheaded with 24 from Terry Ashby before retiring, the refreshments served on the ground seemed to have left a strange silence in their wake, as it has been very hard getting any other details of the play, but everyone enthused about the ensuing social whirl in the Cavern where some 200 enjoyed the Disco and refreshments.
O, Cricket lovely Cricket !
··· ··· ··· ··· ··· ··· ···

Personality of the Month

MONTY - WE SALUTE YOU!

Mr. Alfred G. ('Monty') Webb retired from Wethereds at the end of last month after 32 years' service in various departments with the company, which he joined in 1945.

FREE TRADE RULES OK

J.M. (JOE) SAUNDERS
SALES DEVELOPMENT MANAGER, FREE TRADE DEPARTMENT.

Joe, who has not been seen around the Brewery of late, has been receiving one to those fashionable new hip joints at a Windsor Nursing home. We understand that he is now back on his feet after a successful 'op' and should be out of hospital this week with the assistance of crutches. We all hope to see you before Christmas, Joe.

'HIP - HIP'

BRIAN NORTH, WINE / SPIRIT WAREHOUSE MANAGER.

Brian seems to have liked the result of his first 'Hip-op' so much that he returned to the 'theatre' for an encore on the other hip. He is at present recovering in Wycombe hospital and should make a 'spirited' return very soon.

'Get Hip' in November.

For the record, we notice that Jack Cook started this hip fashion last November. (Wethered 'News' -

Sadly, Stan died and the paper finished after only 19 copies in June 1979.

Wethered's were not into advertising in a big way, mainly using newspapers. The author has never seen any water jugs or trays, but this 1938 cinema foyer is full of adverts!

Left: a very nice quirky comic postcard.

Right: a very rare Bakelite ash tray

This advert was usually found in football programmes.

Pictured at the Wellington Arms Hotel in Stratfield Saye. The two lorries here being used as coaches are 'Progress' and 'Advance', if it wasn't too far a distance the employees would travel on the back of the lorries for their outing.

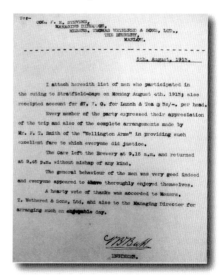

A list of employees who went on the outing and on the right a letter of thanks to Col. Stevens from Victor Butt. In 1932, the directors decided that "owing to the serious effect of the beer tax" they did not feel justified in contributing towards an annual outing. The usual time however would be allowed off and it was hoped that employees would enjoy themselves as much as possible in the vicinity of Marlow.

'ADVANCE'

The 1913 outing to Goring, with ladies as well going on this particular trip. Other outings included Bournemouth in June 1921. It took 3 lorries and one car to carry all the employees and the company gave a donation of £50.

In June 1924 an outing to Wembley, too late for the cup final but presumably to view the remnants of the 1923 Exhibition. Weymouth was the destination in 1925, a telegram was sent expressing thanks to all the employees.

Then there was the infamous outing to France, when five didn't make the ferry home. Basil Tegg decided to show the others a church where he was a P.O.W. in the Second World War.

LIST OF EMPLOYEES GOING TO GORING-ON-THAMES.
Saturday August 23rd, 1913.

Mrs. Anson,	W. Portlock
,, Rockell.	W. E. Nott.
,, Furmston.	J. Lennard.
,, Clark.	C. Grainger.
,, Allen.	C. Furmston.
,, Grainger.	A. Aldouse.
,, Moody.	W. Glanville.
,, Sewell.	H. Smith. Junr.
,, Beldon.	P. Vye.
,, Stacey.	C. Hewitt.
,, Cook.	W. Didcock.
,, Swadling.	W. Herbert.

They went further and further inland from Dunkirk, then found a café where, as the story goes, someone recognised him and there were drinks all round with little thought of the time. Eventually they remembered the ferry, but when they got back to Dunkirk all they could see was everybody waving at them and the funnels of the vessel. They managed to sneak back home on Sunday as they only had day passports. This was a Dunkirk celebration day.

Stan Turner   Jim Thorne   Eric Rollings   Basil Tegg   Charlie Thorne

THE BREWERY'S DAY TRIP TO FRANCE, THIS TIME EVERYONE RETURNED ON TIME!

Here are two that got there and back: painters John Atkins and George Fradgley with a background of the magnificent Calais Town Hall.

Here's Tommy with his mode of transport for his brushes as he didn't drive.

Harry Langley is in the middle fast asleep. On the right also asleep is Tommy Goodall, a drayman who was also a part time chimney sweep, or maybe it was the other way round!

Amongst some of the trips the brewery organised was this one to Guinness at Park Royal, London, in January 1966. *Back row:* Guinness rep., Peter Castree, Keith Hewlett, bus driver John White. *Middle row:* Jim McNab, John Curry, Paul Sykes, Bernie Carvell, Daryl Sherwin, Roger Etherington. *Front row:* Mick Hall, Keith Butler, David Gregory, Jim Hunter.

Another Guinness trip, this one in April 1978. *Back row:* Dacre Newman, Malcolm Edwards, Stan Ridge, Dave Shurlock, (Guinness rep). *Front row:* Dave Evans, Derek Gibbs, Brian Boulton, (Guinness rep).

The Brewhouse staff lining up at Morland's Brewery, Abingdon, in February 1984.

A trip to Whitbread's hop farm at Paddock Wood, Kent. In the background are Oast houses for drying hops. *From the left:* Trevor Painter, Ian Irvine, Bob Tuffrey, Keith Hewlett and Paul Flint.

Right: Andy Ross, Derek Painter, Keith Hewlett, Melvyn Deri and Ian Irvine.

'Progress' dressed up for Hospital Sunday, when they would parade around town holding buckets for donations, as the local Marlow hospital was run on charity money. Francis Owen Wethered is on the left, V. Butt and Jack Lennard Snr. right. Circa 1912

'Advance', *above,* and 'Perseverance', *right,* dressed in the brewery yard. *Left:* Jack Lennard Snr, V Butt with sash with Francis Owen Wethered on the back.

One of the earliest photos of the brewery being used for a carnival. As you come under the arch from the High Street there is still a covered area on the right, it was used as an open dray shed. As you can see on the left there is a horse drawn dray. *From the left:* Dorothy Lennard, unknown, May Lennard, Victorine Lennard. On the right you can see Lily Shaw, who later worked in the mineral store and married Jack Lennard.

Wethered's were frequently asked to donate money for various local good causes. Here are just some of the donations made…

- In 1906 one guinea to Beaconsfield Fire Brigade towards the cost of a new fire engine.
- Subscription to Marlow Regatta in 1913.
- Wooburn Working Men's Club donation of £1 towards new billiard table in 1913.
- Donated £25, 2½ barrels of beer and 4 firkins of ginger beer to the peace celebrations.
- Marlow Hospital annual subscription of 5 guineas.
- 1925: Donation of £70 to The Cottage Hospital in respect of special services last year to the employees.
- 1928: £20 towards Marlow Church Spire Fund.
- Donated £10 towards Marlow St John's Motor Ambulance.
- £10.10s.0d. to Marlow Rowing Club for their new boat fund in July 1958.

'Victor' being dressed up at Wethered's wood yard in Station Road, known as Parsonage Wharf, and getting ready for the Hospital Sunday Parade.

The Simmonds family are pictured with young Peter Simmonds hanging out of the cab, he later worked at the brewery for 40 years. On the back is a giant swan which was kept in the barn just used for carnivals.

The barn was used to store wood to be used on the pubs; it was cleared of wood in 1958 ready to be sold.

Parsonage Gardens now stands on this site..

Garrett Lennard alongside 'Powerful', opposite the George and Dragon close to Higginson Park. It was a British Legion float with the armed forces represented on the back.

Below, and dressed up on the back of 'Victor,' are members of the Jeannine Greville Dance Academy. They are celebrating William Shakespeare's 400th anniversary in 1964. The Dance Academy is still operating at Henley.

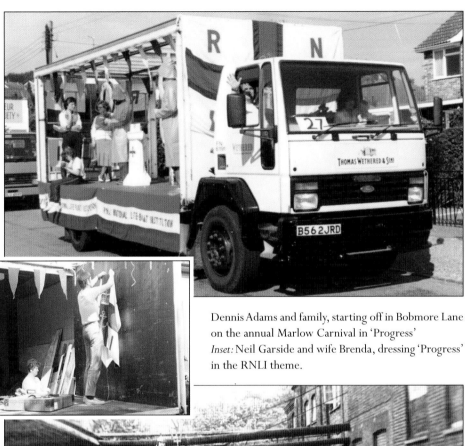

Dennis Adams and family, starting off in Bobmore Lane on the annual Marlow Carnival in 'Progress'
Inset: Neil Garside and wife Brenda, dressing 'Progress' in the RNLI theme.

Another lorry preparing for a procession (around the late 1930's) in the brewery yard. A lady is dressed as Britannia and there is a huge lion on the back, apparently this theme was used fairly regularly. Only two of the five standing in front can be recognised: Garrett Lennard is left, V. Butt in the middle. Quite often Garrett's daughters would play a part on these floats.

The rather eccentric landlord, Dennis Catton, from the Bull at Sonning is on the left next to draymen Pete Hogan and Bobby Gee, with a huge delivery of beer for the Queen's Silver Jubilee. He was hoping to sell 10,688 pints.

It's Dennis once again on his penny farthing; leaning out of the window is Jan Hoare, promoting Winter Royal.

Cheers, 10,688 times

Here's to the Jubilee! And regulars at the Bull Hotel, Sonning, will be able to say that 10,688 times as they raise their glasses of Wethereds " real ale."

For that's the number of pints — equal to 1,336 gallons — that arrived at the hotel from the Marlow brewery in time for the extra licensing hours of the Jubilee next week.

Pictured, from left, with the bumper consignment are hotel staff Mr Kevin Shales, Mrs Veda Stewart, Mrs Louise Lovelace, Mrs Marie Kinge, Mrs Gwen Catton, Mr Dennis Catton (licensee), and draymen Mr Pete Hogan and Mr Robert Gee.

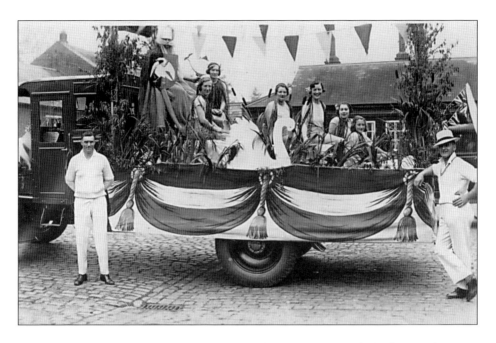

Both lorries have been prepared in the brewery yard. The six ladies on the back are with a swan, which is Marlow's familiar symbol.

Waiting at the Causeway outside the George and Dragon to take part in the parade up the High Street in 1935. Jack Lennard is the driver on the left and driver's mate sitting is Jack Edwards.

On the far table in the middle is Billy Whitbread with Brian Boulton to his left and Peter Sparks on his right.

After dinner there was a competition to guess the total service years, added up, of those present. The closest to the correct number won a bottle of whisky.

Left to right, Jack Lennard, Fred Boddy, Frank Wye, Accountant John Hodginson, Managing Director Mike Gregory, Transport Manager Tony Wilkinson, and George Levie.

Must be at least a 1000 years service between all of them!

An annual dinner was held at The George and Dragon, and latterly at the Cavern Club, for employees with 20 or more years service. It was known as the 20/40 Club. *Above* are Frank Towers, Keith Hewlett and Bill Clark.

Two engineers having a good chinwag: Arthur Coventry, *left,* who took over the Chief Engineer's job when Victor Butt retired, and Keith Hewlett, *right,* who was also an engineer and one of a number of employees who came from Strong's Brewery at Romsey.

Left to right, ex-draymen Jack Cook, Bill Mudie, with workers from the front office, Cyril Moores and Alf Fuller. Alf had come from Higg's Brewery at Reading and often played drums in a group at The Britannia.

Three Wethered employees receiving their twenty year presentations from three different Whitbread chairmen.

The author, with his wife Beryl, receiving silver tray, decanter and glasses from Sir Samuel Whitbread, Chairman 1984-92.

On the right, Wally Griffin with his wife Marge receiving his watch from Sir Charles Tidbury who was Chairman from 1978-84.

Left, Jack Cook with his son in law, George Malster receiving his watch from Alex Bennett, Chairman 1971-78.

In the nineteen twenties when very few people could afford quality cameras, superb postcards were published like the example above by Greville of Marlow. It shows how Col. Stevens and a fellow Wethered's Director realised the importance of providing recreational facilities, but it was only after a petition signed by the staff that the management agreed.

The story unfolds way back in 1895 when Col. O.P. Wethered personally purchased 5,803 acres of land between Pound Lane and the River Thames for £1500. He then leased it to Marlow Cricket Club at a rent of £20 p.a. for 21 years, it had obviously been done as a gesture of goodwill.

The Pavilion shown in the postcard above was added and a 6ft oak fence erected on three sides. After the conclusion of WW1 Marlow struggled to find players and in 1920 briefly folded. About the same time O.P. Wethered died and the executors decided to put the land up for sale for £1200. On the 6th July 1920 a total of 54 staff (just over half) signed a petition to the directors requesting it be purchased by the brewery as a recreation club. Within two weeks it met with the board's approval and they suggested the organisation be put in the hands of a committee representing all employees for a period of two years. The matter would then be reconsidered and sold if necessary. In addition they immediately spent £300 on upgrading the Pavilion as a Social club, and a further £91was paid to the Marlow Gas Co. for gas installation.

They did not approve the installation of electricity or a gramophone, but purchased a second hand piano instead. It meant of course that Wethered's Cricket team which had been formed in 1905 could continue playing home fixtures in Pound Lane, much better than their previous arrangement with Marlow C.C. The venture was such a success that at a board meeting on 7th May 1926 it was approved that a groundsman be employed at not more than £2 per week, with stamps paid by the company.

Although the Cricket team did have fixtures against local teams such as Frieth and Wooburn, soon after WW2 it became difficult to raise a regular team and on the 5th May 1959 Marlow Sports Club was given a 14 year lease at a nominal rent. Marlow's stature grew, and they even got promoted to the Home Counties League for a while and hosted many Bucks Minor Counties matches prior to a leaner spell. Under Whitbread's ownership the future is now very questionable.

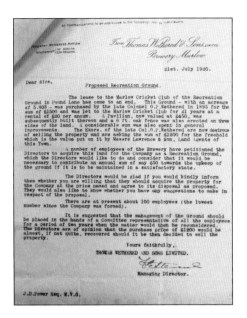

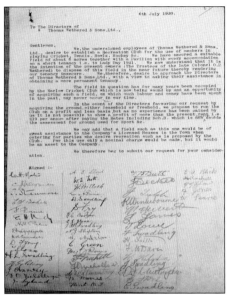

These are original letters asking the brewery to buy a recreation ground for the employees. The letter on the left states that the lease to Marlow Cricket Club had expired and the executors of the late Colonel O.P. Wethered would be willing to sell the ground. The letter on the right is the petition signed by the employees.

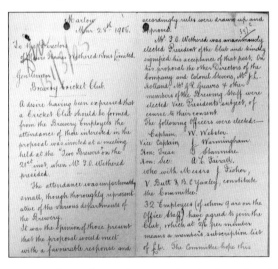

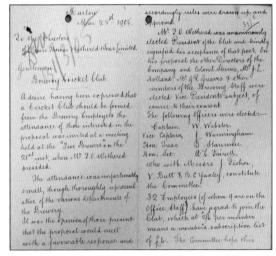

The two letters above state that they have elected F. O. Wethered as President of the Cricket Club and are forming a committee with 32 employees who agreed to join the club. An offer to play on Star Meadow (now Green Verges and Heron's Place housing estate) had been received at £2 per annum, the committee being told they would not get a better offer and felt it would bring the employees closer together. H Turner was employed as Groundsman in 1926 at a wage of £2 per week.

The brewery cricket team was formed in 1905, after a meeting at the George and Dragon. The brewery donated £2.2s.0d in 1906. This was the team in the early 1920's. V. Butt would seem to be the umpire, with Harry Hillsdon, W.O. Swadling, and Jack Lennard Snr. in the middle

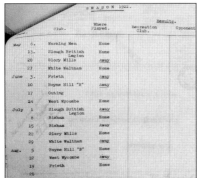

Above left is the fixture list from 1922. *Above right* is the team in 1932. *Back row:* W. E. Nott, R. J. Walker, T. Barnard, G. W. Levie, W. J. Walder, A. Coventry, *Front row:* R. Anderson, F. Swadling, H.H. Palmer, F. Brooks, J. Lennard,

The Ladies' team has just beaten the men 118 to 86, but there again the ladies were playing with only two stumps!

The Ladies' team from 1972: Jackie Collins, Sue Jones, Margaret Probert, Mrs A Du Celliee Muller, Linda Ellison, Barbara Thain, Leslie Payne, Linda Swadling, Carol Franklin, Margaret Dobner. Francis Arnold.

Each year the brewery would invite the tenants, managers and wives to a cricket match and would serve refreshments. Half of them came for the first game in June and the rest for the second game in August.

BREWERS' PARTY FOR TENANTS

Value Of Marlow "Get-Together"

CRICKET MATCH

MESSRS. Thomas Wethered and Sons, Ltd., of the Brewery, Marlow, entertained one half of the tenants of their licensed houses on Wednesday last week, practically 120 people being present.

A cricket match was played between the Brewery XI and an XI got up by the tenants, which resulted in a win for the tenants.

At the tea which followed, in a marquee on the brewery recreation ground, a few words of welcome were addressed to the tenants by the chairman, Colonel J. R. Wethered, D.S.O., who stated how pleased he was to have that opportunity of personally talking to people whom ordinarily it was only possible to see occasionally. He felt that the "get together" would tend to bring the tenants and the management of the brewery closer together when constructive criticisms could be considered and suggestions put forward for their mutual benefit.

In reply, Mr. A. V. Gregory, licensee of the "Shaggy Calf," Slough, thanked Colonel Wethered for his hospitality.

Mr. F. Edwards of the "Pond House" Reading, replied on behalf of the tenants to the chairman's welcome and said he felt sure he was expressing the views of the whole party when he said how much they appreciated the friendly gesture that had been made. The proceedings closed on a happy note with assurances on both sides that an invitation would be issued next year and accepted.

Messrs. Wethered propose entertaining the remaining half of their tenants in a similar way on August 31st.

The scores for the cricket match were:

TENANTS' XI.

F. Newell, b G. Davis, 52; A. V. Gregory, b Morris, 4; K. R. Ford, b Morris, 0; R. Lavender, b Morris, 0; T. W. Story, c Palmer, b Walker, 29; H. Allin, b Walker, 0; H. Neville, b Walker, 5; F. J. Brazier, c Morris, b Davis, 0; R. Plumridge, not out, 1; J. A. Thomas, not out, 1; extras, 4; total, 96.

W. E. Curtis did not bat.

BREWERY XI.

J. Harvey, lbw, b Plumridge, 4; F. Nicholls, c Newell, b Plumridge, 11; G. W. Levie, b Lavender, 2; G. Davis, b Lavender, 1; D. A. H. Russell, c Lavender, b Story, 5; R. J. Walker, b Newell, 4; W. F. Morris, c Brazier, b Newell, 2; W. G. Moody, run out, 1; H. H. Palmer, c Gregory, b Newell, 8; H. Samuelson, not out, 5; P. Willmott, b Ford, 0; extras, 1; total, 44.

The tenants won by 52 runs on this occasion in June 1938 and also won again in August.

Stanley Garton the Managing Director, had been trying for three years to organise a get together for all the employees. Now the war had finished the time was right, so a committee was formed. They organised (amongst other things) a Punch and Judy show, conjurer, pony rides, races for children and adults, an assortment of sideshows and a comic football match.

Sports events were none too serious, prizes were donated by the company, with a concert and dancing taking place in the evening.

Nearly three hundred attended the party; they were entertained to tea with plenty of ice cream for the children. Mr. Garton was pleased the employees had accepted him as one of the family, and thanked them very much, he was also proud of them for turning up in such strength on VJ days. The conjuring entertainment was given by Mr Jack White and radio programme by Mr F Lowe.

Derrick Barratt, winner of the Under Fives race, looks older to me!

Wally Griffin won the apple and Bucket race, then beat Nobby Mitchell up in a Pillow Fight.

Mrs Jones, winner of the Egg and Spoon race.

Check out the results

Children's Races

Winners of the children's races were as follows :
Under 5 years, boys—1 Derrick Barratt, 2 David Stevens ; girls—1 Valerie Jones, 2 Jacqueline Lennard, 3 Jennifer Lennard. Under 10 years, boys—1 George Aldous, 2 Raymond Langley, 3 Victor Barratt ; girls—1 Mavis Stone, 2 Barbara Edwards, 3 Doreen Edwards. Under 14 years, boys—1 Alfred Aldous, 2 John Hillsdon, 3 Christopher Power ; girls—1 Pamela Jones, 2 Georgina Aldous, equal 3 Ivy Paine, Ann Langley, Joyce Moody.
Under 18 years, boys—1 Kenneth Howard, 2 Robert Carter, Ronald Swadling. Three-legged race—1 Pamela Jones and Joyce Moody, 2 Gary Lennard and Robert Carter, 3 Georgina Aldous and Ellen Hillsdon. Egg and spoon—1 John Hillsdon, 2 Ronald Swadling, 3 Gary Lennard ; girls—1 Pamela Jones, 2 Ellen Hillsdon, 3 Mavis Stone.

Adult Races

Winners of adult races were : Egg and spoon, ladies—1 Mrs. Jones, 2 Mrs. Cook, 3 Mrs. Simmons ; men—1 J. Edwards, 2 A. Coventry, 3 J. Cook. Thread needle—1 Mrs. Jones, 2 Mrs. Griffin. Apple and bucket—1 W. Griffin, 2 H. Langley, 3 F. Brooks. Three-legged race—1 H. Langley and Mrs. Faulkner, 2 Mr. Palmer and Mrs. Sizeland, 3 Mr. Guttridge and Miss Guttridge.
Under 40 years, men—1 J. Edwards, 2 H. Bowles, 3 A. Wing. Under 50 years, men—1 H. Langley, 2 W. Moody, 3 A. Coventry. Over 50 years, men—1 A. Eaton, 2 F. Willis, 3 Mr. Palmer. Under 40 years, ladies—1 Miss Guttridge, 2 Miss Easton, 3 Mrs. Griffin. Under 50 years, ladies—1 Mrs. Power, 2 Mrs. Bond, 3 Mrs. Norman. Over 50 years, ladies—1 Mrs. Sizeland, 2 Mrs. Faulkner, 3 Mrs. Batt. Pillow fight—1 Mr. Griffin, 2 A. Mitchell.

Competitions

The bowls competitions prizewinners were : 1 G. J. Lennard and F. Brooks ; 2 N. Anderson and A. Carter ; 3 W. Moody and T. Golding ; 15th end, rink 1, W. Faulkner and A. Wing ; 15th end, rink 4, E. Blick and W. Griffiths ; travelling voucher, W. Moody and T. Golding ; "bowlers' grave," score 13, H. Moores and A. Mitchell ; starters on rink 4, H. Stacey, C. Simmons, F. Swadling and W. Rixon.
Putting competition prizewinners were : 1 Mrs. Brook ; equal 2 Mrs. H. Langley, Mrs. Flint, Mrs. Rixon ; consolation, Mr. A. Lee, Mr. L. Stevens, Mr. J. Jones ; most ones, 1 Mr. H. Langley, 2 F. Swadling, 3 A. Lee ; Novelty, 1 Mrs. Nott, 2 J. Jones, highest number for any hole, J. Hillsdon ; lowest, first half, C. Jones ; lowest second half, C. Jones ; lowest score (lady), Mrs. Moores and Mrs. Rixon ; lowest score, men, C. Jones ; highest score, Mr. Power ; most threes, 1 Mr. Griffin, 2 Mr. Stepton, 3 Mrs. Levie ; longest sequence of any number, equal 1 Mrs. Levie and Mr. Swadling, 2 D. White.

Back row left to right: H. Langley, R. Flint, J. Cook, B. Faulkner, A. Carter, W. Griffin, C. Symonds, F. Willis, H. Shipton and F. Brooks. *Middle row:* J. Steptoe, R. Anderson, F. Swadling, F. Mitchell, C. Jones, J. Lennard Snr, J. Jones, A. Coventry, B. Mudie, J. Lennard Jnr. *Front row:* T. Golding, A. Wing G. Levie, T. Childs, H. Moores, S. Garton, P. Power, V. Butt, E. Blick, H. Stacy, B. Rixon, J. Edwards.

Party Time for the children of employees

Some of the kids at the front include: Tom, Derek, Terry & John Barratt, Ray Langley, George and Alf Aldous, Rosa Davison, Edwina Gutteridge, Margaret Fountain, Jean North, Mavil Stone, Patsy Steptoe and one of the girls on the pony, Barbara Edwards

A very sporting Head Brewer Paul Thompson playing tennis and hockey.

Not all the names, but at the back (in no particular order), 'Doodle' Swadling, Bill Barratt (with fez), Harry Frith, Fred Barber, Alice Munday, Jack Cook, John Bond, Boddy, Mabel Wing and Albert 'Rabbit' Wing. Middle: Lady on the left Fanny Blick, in the middle of the row Granny Winterbourne. Some of the children in the front row: Jenny Lennard, Barbara Edwards, Jean Barratt, Ivy Paine, Ena Alldous, Ellen Hillsdon, Joyce Moody, Ray Langley, George Alldous, Bill Wing, John Barratt

WETHERED'S DINNER.—The second annual dinner and prize distribution of Messrs. T. Wethered and Sons' Recreation Club, organised by the bowls section, was held at the Railway Hotel on Saturday with Mr. O. B. Butt in the chair. Mrs. Butt presented the various awards gained during the season to the following: Marlow Cup runner-up, Mr. J. Tubb; ladies' singles (presented by Mrs. Jakeman), Mrs. Yates; 2, Mrs. Lennard, sen.; men's singles — 1, J. Jones; 2, W. G. Moody; singles handicap, F. W. Brooks and C. N. Moores; 2 (equal), F. Rockell, A. J. West, and A. J. Shipton; ladies' putting championship (prize given by Mrs. Wethered), Mrs. Brooks. A pipe was presented to Mr. C. Simmons, who drives the members to their away games. Following the dinner the gathering, numbering nearly 70, enjoyed an entertainment by Messrs. Fox and Jackson, E. Neighbour, A. Grevatt, F. G. Ponting, N. Turner and J. Edwards (pianist).

Jack Lennard taking aim.

In the middle is Terry Ashby, third from right is Keith Budd, with Wally Griffin and Ken 'Shadow' Bowles. This photo was in the Whitbread era when they would take on teams from other breweries, it made for a nice weekend away.

From the left: Fred Simmonds, Jim McNab, Mike Gregory, Dick Cooper, Gordon Tandy, Pete Slade, and Tony Wilkinson. In the middle and centre of attention is 'Barleycorn Keg', so called after Strong's Keg Bitter. 'BK' used to run at Slough, but was about as good as some of the Cricket teams and never won a race!

Arthur Moody and Malcolm Edwards with the cup,
Kelvin Gryckiewicz, Tanny Swadling, Jan Hoare, Charlie Symes, Tom Barratt, Archie Rockall, Asa Biggs and 'Shadow' Bowles

One of the teams that played against the managers and tenants.
Back row includes: Pete Sparks, Tom Barratt, John Harris. *Next row down includes:* Dixie Dean, Dave Mansfield, Bob Corke. *Centre includes:* 'Shadow', Dennis Gillett, Jan. *Bottom row includes:* Bernie Carvell, Keith Jessop, Jack Cook, Dave Lee Missing names are managers/tenants.

Enjoying free beer and food

Sheila Warne, Fred Jolly, with Stan Ridge, on the far right.

Back row: Tom Barrett, Dennis Gillett, Tony Wilkinson, Brian Hammond, David Evans, Graham Miles, Stuart Deri, Bob Pritchard, Paul West, Billy Whitbread, Ken 'Shadow' Bowles,

Front row: Jock Irvine, Jim Greig, Brian Bowles, John Murphy, Bob Miles, Nigel North, Bish, Dave Moore, George How, Bob Gee.

Back row: Graham Pritchard, David Evans, Derrick Pritchard, Graham Miles, Dave Bradley, Brian Hammond and Manager Dennis Gillett. *Front row:* Steve Maddran, Peter Austin, Nigel North, Dick Porter (with trophy), Jock Irvine, Bernie Hall, in June 1973.

Inset: Nigel and Dick, with a cake for winning the league.

Originally it was a very basic cellar which was used for storing empty beer crates. Shortly after bottling ceased, the brewery workers formed a social club, at first having to use the function room of the Clayton Arms and also Marlow Rugby Club. After much discussion, the management agreed to hand over the cellar. Most of the work was carried out voluntarily with some money being donated by the company. The results were outstanding …

AFTER … THE LOUNGE BAR

David Hobgen, *below,* the last steward, studying horse racing form in the dance hall bar. When the Cavern Club closed he went on to manage a betting shop.

Parties were held at the George and Dragon, and later at the Cavern Club, Father Christmases included Head Brewer Bill Fisher, and drayman John Keith, neither of these needed any padding! There was also John Harris; he did need padding but not a wig! The kids would always receive a lovely present.

Bill Fisher, *above,* with some of the kids enjoying the party: Keith Butler, Keith Tubb, Michael Thorne, Linda Simmonds, Tony David, Mick Rockall and Rod Farrell.

Alongside are details of a very early party held at the Two Brewers, Marlow, in 1909, the Truss family being the landlords at that time. 140 dinners are indicated at 2/6d (12½ pence) each meal. A gallon of beer was only 1/4d (7½ pence). They certainly could drink, as they got through 54 gallons. Even packets of cigarettes were given away. Pensioners and widows were also invited.

Desmond 'Dizzle' North messing about as usual, and John Atkins with his wife next to him, this time at the George and Dragon, Marlow.

Standing: John 'Snowy' Austin, Gordon Young, Cliff Budd, Pete Greggs, Keith Hewlett, Tony Wilkinson, Ray Evans, Derek Brown, Ken Mansfield. In front: Dave Lovering and Andy Ross. Winners in the first season of the Wethered dart league.

THE CAVERN LADIES' TEAM

Left to right: Linda Ellison, Linda Swadling, Eileen McMillan, Jill Langley, Carol Franklin, Liz Bridge, Yvonne Steptoe, Ursula Frost, Les Tunney, Sheila Warne, Ann Tandy, Ann Provost.

THE CAVERN SPORTS & SOCIAL CLUB

DARTS EVENING

with Special Guest
CLIFF LAZARENKO

Thursday, 26th March, 1981

8 p.m. to 11 p.m.   Ticket: £2.00

An exhibition darts evening with giant professional darts player, Big Cliff Lazarenko, taking on all-comers. This proved a very popular evening, seen here with Ken Mansfield.

Another top professional player, Wee Jockey Wilson also appeared in the Cavern, seen with Les Tunney on the left and Linda Swadling

Frank Steptoe and Lillian Budd counting money from the fruit machines, this had to be done regularly due to a couple of break-ins.

There were two snooker tables, one of which came from Harleyford. On a Saturday morning a group of employees went out to Harleyford, dismantled it and brought it back to the Cavern. The other table came from Whitbread's social club in Chiswell Street, London, both were very popular and there was often a 'cue' to play.

Just a few of the top acts that appeared at the Cavern Club in the last few years before closure

Clockwise from above: The Wurzels; Roger De Courcey and Nookie Bear; Chas and Dave, with Wilkie in the middle; The Swinging Blue Jeans; Mick Miller and Jimmy Jones.

Jack Frost (hiding!), Heather Pritchard, Sharon Dimbleby, Linda Swadling, Glen North and Ursula Frost Smartly dressed Cavern 'bar staff' for Christmas.

Fancy dress for New Year: Mike Tingey (Batman), Linda Swadling (Robin), Heather Pritchard (Catwoman), Glen North (Joker).

The Foster Family are propping up the bar - John, Peter and Ernie. 'Dob' Taylor is at the other end. The Steward is Dave Hobgen.

Melvyn Deri, Wilkie, Keith Hewlett, Jan Hoare and Derek Painter.

Included here is John Smart, Bill Turner, Chris Flint and Nigel North.

Clockwise from top left: (1) Michelle Durrant, Beryl Evans, Simon Durrant, Matt Evans. (2), Jim Parker, with Tanny (seated). (3) Three members of the darts team - Pete and Alan Bowles with Dave Walker behind. (5) Associate member Pat Ryan with wife Jenny. (5) David Barlow, Ian Campbell and Pete Hogan.

Eddie Walker, John Smart, Bill Turner, Nigel North, Paul Flint and Pat 'Patch' Olney.

Phil 'Squirrel' Howard and his wife Imelda, with Roy 'Rupe' Woodward.

Chris Bridge, Bob Tuffrey, Andy Greig and Glen North.

The little brown Willys now sprayed red is advertising Sam Whitbread beer. This photo was taken at Whitbread's Estate, Southill Park in Bedfordshire and shows ex England cricketers going around the Whitbread circuit in the South of England for charity. This was organised by ex-England wicket keeper, Jim Parks, who at the time worked for Whitbreads. Players are (not quite all): Alan Oakman, Tom Cartwright, Fred Titmus, John Snow, Basil D'Oliveira, Jim Parks, Robin Hobbs and David Allen.

OBJ with Morris dancers at a pub in the New Forest

These three vintage lorries regularly visited steam rallies, carnivals and school fetes throughout the summer from April to the end of September.

The lorry on the right, a Thornycroft J type, needs little introduction. Bought in 1921 and used until 1946 when it was returned to Thornycroft to show in their museum, it was returned back to Wethered's in 1969.

Victor, shown in the middle, a Thornycroft Sturdy arrived in 1946 and after its working life was sold to a local farmer at Lane End. It was then rescued and restored by Peter Davies who sold it back to Wethered's around 1977.

On the left, a 1928 Willys Crossley Overland which started off as a baker's van but was converted for advertising purposes. It was known as the little brown lorry and had a unique number plate, OBJ 1, which was the name of a beer brewed by Dutton's of Blackburn "OH BE JOYFUL"

Unfortunately, the lorries were all sold, the Willys is back in Lancashire, and the two Wethered lorries probably couldn't be any further from Marlow as they are now both in Cumbria.

Plaques, as those shown right, were often given for attending steam rallies. Instead of mounting them on a board, the author thought it would be a novel idea to mount them on a barrel.

An unusual photo, as we usually got towed off the rally field after heavy rain, but in this instance we were being towed onto the field! It turned out to be one of our better days as we stayed in the beer tent most of the time with free beer, food and music.

MP tours brewery

High Wycombe Conservative M.P. Ray Whitney, presenting limited number framed prints of "Perseverance" for appreciation of the good work carrid out on the vintage vehicles. These prints were sketched by a brother of one of the reps.

Left to right: Charlie Symes, Archie Rockall, Ray Whitney, Keith Hewlett, Wally Griffin, the author, Robin Woodage and Jan Hoare.

TV's Miss Marple, starring Joan Hickson who celebrated her 80th birthday the day before this filming. Peter Tilbury is behind. Picture taken to the rear of The Bear, Woodstock for an episode called Nemesis.

The Darling Buds of May taken at Sheppard Neame Brewery, Faversham.

In the middle Philip Franks who also starred in Heartbeat

The author with 'Perseverance' outside London's Old Bailey – a true life drama.

'Perseverance' in the workshop having an overhaul before embarking on a gruelling two week tour of the Whitbread depots around England. First week around the South, week two up North, marking Whitbread's 250 years of brewing, and also to raise money for charity.

Outside Liverpool FC with the eternal flame in the background for the memory of the fans who lost their lives in the Hillsborough disaster.

Outside Burnley FC after a stop at the Blackburn depot overnight. The author, a big Burnley fan, could not resist this photo.

The changeover point for some of the drivers. For the second week the author swapped over with Mick Mitchell who is bottom right.

A very impressive cavalcade outside the offices of the Boddington's Brewery in Manchester.

The gruelling two week tour of England finally finished up at the Whitbread head office, Chiswell Street, East London.

John Lawless, the leading drayman with horses 'Hengist' and 'Horsa' who first appeared on 1st Nov 1976. This became an annual visit when promoting Winter Royal, and was a big hit with the landlords and a showstopper in the High Street.

Jean and Mick Lowe of the Britannia, Marlow, who went on to run the Jack of Newbury at Binfield.

A Whitbread drayman leading the horses up the High Street. For years Whitbread only had Grey Shire Horses. Following in the Wethered's tradition, all their horses had distinctive names.

Rhoda and Jim Tubb were tenants at the Plough, Marlow for a number of years. Jim's father, Joe *(inset)*, was a member of the winning team of drivers in the lorry competition in the 1920's.

Wethered's had the chance to purchase the breweries below but declined for some reason or other…

CANNON BREWERY, READING, 1901.

DOWSETT BREWERY AND TAP, READING, 1906.

FINN'S BREWERY, NEWBURY.

BAKER, POWELL & CO., WOKINGHAM BREWERY, 1911, WITH 11 PUBS.

BERKHAMSTED BREWERY WITH 42 PUBS.

DONNINGTON BREWERY 1913.

IVES HENLEY BREWERY, WITH 3 PUBS, BUT NOT VIABLE.

One was the Argyle, Market Square, Henley, The Swan, Greys Hill, and another, The Hope, which was right next door to a Wethered pub the Royal Oak, Knowl Hill.

HEADINGTON & SON, ANOTHER WOKINGHAM BREWERY, 1919.

GORING BREWERY, 1924.

This was considered to be too far away. After buying the Farriers Arms, Upper Basildon from Bird's Brewery it was sold almost at once to Gundry's for £775 in 1913.

HEWITTS, WALTHAM ST. LAWRENCE, 1927

WITH 31 FREEHOLD AND 16 LEASE, BUT THERE WAS NO BID.

WELLERS DECLINED 1929

WATLINGTON

Locals at the Victoria pub at Henley reported that the beers were not very good.

Pictured above is The Tudor Arms, which is just down the road from Reading railway station. Bird's Brewery Reading, 17 Caversham Road, was taken over in 1913 at a cost of £11,700. This added nine licensed houses. Bird's were brewing ten different draught beers, and in addition to extra stout had brilliant beer and bitter in bottles. Wethered's had to borrow £5,000 from Lloyds Bank, and pay back at 4½% interest.

A list of the Pubs …
Tudor Arms
Borough Arms
Carpenters Arms
Bridge House, Binfield
Three Frogs, Wokingham
Farriers Arms, Upper Basildon

Leased …
Brewery Tavern
Bricklayers Arms
Gardeners Arms
Weldale Stores

After buying the brewery they used it as the Reading Agency. In 1911 it was selling 1500 barrels per annum.

Above: Just beyond the horse and cart is the pub, The Harrow. Sadly, it is now closed. Through the archway is the brewery with a stag on top. At one end of the street is the pub the Brewery Tap later renamed the Stag; William's Brewery was also known as the Stag Brewery.

This attractive bottle label was issued by the Royal Stag Brewery and is reproduced here by kind permission of the county record office at Aylesbury. The brewery also had pale ale in bottles.

A view from the other end of the street with the Stag and the Brewery on the left.

Strong's of Romsey was another brewer who expanded by buying up smaller brewers and were a fairly big brewer at the time Whitbread's took over in 1969. They had a workforce of nearly 700 employees, and a fleet of 44 delivery vehicles which was double Wethered's fleet.

They had a bottling hall capable of filling 30,000 bottles an hour, and a kegging plant filling 120 ten gallon kegs per hour.

Although Strong's seemed to invest a lot of money there was not much spent at Wethered's. Ironically, the last brew on 26 June 1981 was Whitbread Trophy.

Strong's transport lined up in the brewery yard.

Queen's Head, Bradfield Strange of Aldermaston was taken over along with 50 pubs by Strong's of Romsey in 1949 and transferred them over to Wethered's in 1950. All transferred assets and liabilities amounted to a figure of £190,950 Also two draymen would bring up a dray daily whilst in the process of changing over.

The Pineapple at Brimpton was an attractive thatched roof pub belonging to Strange's Brewery, but shown here after the takeover in Wethered's livery with the local fox hunt.

The Newmarket public house in Newbury closed in 1971 and received £8,100 compensation.

The Ship, Ashford Hill sold in 1972 for £14,500. To date it still remains in the same family, when the virginia creeper is cut back from the front of the pub in winter the Wethereds' sign can still be seen.

Higgs of Reading had only 8 pubs, and were taken over in 1953. They were also known as the Lion Brewery from Castle Street.

Although the beers were brewed by Wethered's, following the takeover, the continued use of the Higgs trade mark kept faith with the local drinkers. The beer was also bottled in Reading.

202

One of a number of Thornycroft lorries being loaded at Chiswell Street, London, with a horse drawn dray visible in the background. The Whitbread advert on the right dates from the early sixties.

Whitbread's were established in 1742. Samuel Whitbread set up a brewery at Chiswell Street, London, with brothers Godfrey and Thomas Shewell. By 1761 Godfrey had left and Thomas retired, leaving Samuel as the sole proprietor.

Very soon Sam became London's top brewer. In 1761 he was brewing 65,000 barrels; Sam specialised in (Entire) beer - a strong black beer, the raw materials being relatively cheap and was another name for Porter.

He built a new brewery specifically for mass production at Chiswell Street. Expansion was fast, from 1891 to 1914, 48 depots were opened. 1869 saw the introduction of bottled beers. By 1914 more than half the brewery's output of 1 million barrels a year were bottled.

At the beginning of the 1960's through to 1971 Whitbread merged with 23 other breweries, here are just some...Tennant, Dutton's, Cobb, and Brickwood's.

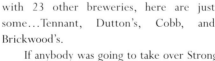

If anybody was going to take over Strong's brewery, it was on the cards that it would be Whitbread, as they had acquired a substantial shareholding in Strong's in 1955.

Early in 1969, Whitbread held some 30% of Strong's shares. They made an offer to acquire the entire share capital of Strong's by means of an exchange of shares in Whitbread. This meant that Wethered's was now under Whitbread's control.

One thing that changed immediately was a wage increase to all employees.

Above: Billy Whitbread, who was a very popular Managing Director at Wethered's mid 1970's.

Owen Peel Wethered, grandson of the founder of the brewery, Thomas Wethered. Owen was born in 1837 and died in 1908. He was educated at Eton and Christ Church Oxford, and was the first chairman of the company 1899 -1908.

Owen, and his brother Thomas, were instrumental in bringing the railway to Marlow in 1873.

Owen joined the Bucks Volunteer Rifle Battalion in 1859 as a Private and became Honorary Colonel in 1886

Some of the posts held by Owen included Director of Marlow Gas Co. Ltd., President of Marlow Cottage Hospital, J.P. for Buckinghamshire and Governor of Sir William Borlase School

Francis Owen Wethered below was a partner from 1890 to1899, and a Director from 1899 to 1922. He took over Chairmanship on the death of his father in 1908 where he remained until his death in Tenerife in 1922. He was also

educated at Eton and Christ Church Oxford and was a famous Oxford Blue who rowed for Oxford against Cambridge in 1885, 86 and 87. After leaving Oxford, he went on to become captain of Marlow Rowing Club. He was a J.P. and also Deputy Lieutenant for Bucks and Lieutenant Colonel of the Bucks Battalion.

Marlow Company Bucks Rifle Volunteers circa 1900. Several of the men are wearing the volunteer long service and good conduct medal introduced in 1894.

David Rush, brewer's clerk, was Marlow's first holder of a Victoria Cross which he gained in the Indian Mutiny on 19th March 1858. Troop Sergeant Major Rush, in company with one other private, attacked 8 of the enemy, who had posted themselves in a Nullah (steep narrow valley) and killed 3 of them. David is buried in All Saints Parish Church, Marlow.

Charles Swain, an engineer, 1900-1917. He was highly regarded at his job by V. Butt; it was only Butt himself that stopped him from becoming Chief Engineer. He came back from the army as an invalid; having been sadly mustard gassed in France whilst fixing a truck. He left in 1917 to join Seabrook's Brewery in Essex as Chief Engineer.

A request for beer by the Marlow Committee for assisting Belgian

Wethered's
ROCKET
Strong Ale

BREWED & BOTTLED BY
WETHERED'S
at the
BREWERY, MARLOW.

David Rush,
1827-1886

refugees was made in October 1914 for a weekly allowance for supply on especially favourable terms.

The committee was providing for 6 families numbering 26 refugees.

JD Power was willing to give through one of the tenants 3 dozen pints of F.P.A. per week.

It was proposed that 3 orders for 1 dozen per week be given to the committee. The beer was to be obtained through one of the Marlow houses. However, it was decided that it would not be appropriate to give beer away or to supply at a lower rate, as it would cause dissatisfaction amongst the local, hard-pressed tenants!

Charles Swain

The building behind these munitions workers was originally used for cask washing, in 1907 it was converted into an engineering shop. Now with the outbreak of war they joined the South Midlands Munitions Committee and entered into contracts to manufacture 3" stokes bombs of which they made 7,037 and more contracts came in 1916.

A total of 3,250 trench bombs were made at a lower rate of 8/9d a bomb; the contract continued for 500 18 pounders mk iii (500 against previously 250). Instructions came from the Ministry to change over from 1200 18 pounder shells at 11/2d each per week to 2000 3" target smoke shells per week at 8/- per shell. It was resolved to acquire the necessary plant to carry out the new contract at a cost of £300.

The contracts proved to be very lucrative, the statement of account showing a nett profit of £2063.11s.0d after paying bonuses. In 1916, V. Butt received a £100 bonus and the men got £40. Nothing was said of the 40 or so women working on the day and night shifts.

In 1917 another bonus came of 20% for V. Butt and 10% to a special employee, who was likely to have been cinema manager, Mr W. J. Dellar. Great credit was given to F. O. Nicholls and the rest of the depleted engineering staff. A total of 61,016 shells were made, and delivered to the bonded warehouse at High Wycombe by their men who were unfit for active service.

Contract No 9: The M D reported that in consequence of the armistice having been signed, he had received from the ministry of munitions, a letter thanking the company and employees for their services and giving 6 weeks to terminate the contract.

Photo taken Christmas 1918, some of the names: *Bottom row:* Newman, Harvey, Coventry, Miss Floss Collins, Ethel Harris. *Second row:* Heatly, Cam, Nicholls, Yates, Dellar, Col. Wethered, Col. Stevens, *Third row:* A Davis, M Davis, Louie Swadling, Miss Walker, G Morris, V Butt (in the middle), M Frith. A Ludgrove, R Perry, E Freshwater, and Stanmore at the end. *Fourth row:* Hilda Saunders, Harvey, Clisby, Cox, Rippington, Grimmet, Harwood, Burnham, Stone. *Back row:* Newman, Plumridge, Udy, Church, Allsworth, May Evans, Dolly Rixon, Eva Hale.

Unveiling War Memorial, Marlow.

The Brewery donated 100 guineas towards the war memorial in memory of four employees who lost their lives:

Sergeant Henry J Haddon, Royal Bucks Hussars, formerly clerical staff killed at Gallipoli August 1916.

Private Robert W Chew, Bucks Battalion died 22 August 1917 aged 23

Private James Frith, Bucks Battalion died 18 July 1916 aged 18, worked in the engineering shop

Private J Gilmore, Lincs Regiment died 22 September 1918 aged 28

A further four men died of sickness:

Major W P Wethered

Private Charles Furmston, Royal Fusiliers died 18 March 1919

Corporal George W Silvey, Royal Berks Regiment died 19 May 1917 aged 33, worked at the brewery for 14 years as a painter

Shoeing Smith Rene A West, Royal Field Artillery died 19 January 1918 aged 40, blacksmith at the brewery for 14 years and also served with Durham L.I. during Boer War.

A further £10 donation was made towards the war memorial in 1921.

In 1900 paid 2/6d a week to the mothers of single men called up by Regiments, this was paid to mothers from the date the men left to join their colours.

By 1917, 81 0f the employees had been in the military.

These two rolls of honour are dedicated to the employees who served in the 1914-18 Great War and to the four employees who lost their lives. The one on the left now hangs appropriately in the Marlow British Legion and was designed by Sir Joseph Causton and amounted to eighteen guineas.

Two former work colleagues, Cyril Henry Moores and Lance Bombardier Ted Bonner met in Greece after being away for 3 years. Both had taken part in the battle of El Alamein and had also seen action in Libya, Tunisia, Sicily and Italy. Cyril served in the Royal Tank Regiment and Ted with the 33 Field Battery of the Royal Artillery. Cyril had been in the Middle East for 4 years and Ted had been abroad for 3 years. Both rejoined the company after the war.

Mr and Mrs E Tubb of 182, Oxford Road received a postcard in 1943. To their relief their youngest son was alive, the card read that George was a prisoner of war in Japanese hands. He was captured at the fall of Singapore on Feb. 15 1942 after only being in the Far East a few months. The card was the first communication they had had in 18 months, George was 26 and had been at the brewery since leaving school, George's father also worked at the brewery as a stoker. After George's release he went on to have seven children.

Colonel Joseph Robert Wethered C.M.G., D.S.O., J. P., gained the Queen's South Africa medal with 4 clasps, King's South Africa medal with 2 clasps and mentioned 6 times in despatches. General Manager in 1926; Chairman and Managing Director in 1927.

He died on the 8th of March 1942 aged 68, brother of Harold Francis Wethered who died at Lucknow, India.

Two years after his death, his son, Major Guy Ernest Fitzgerald Wethered, a brilliant athlete before the war, died of wounds in Burma.

This plaque, right, is in the church at Hurley where his father Florence was vicar.

These three Sergeant Majors have more medals than our local hero Steve Redgrave: From left, G Jakeman (Yard Foreman) T Golding (Bottlery Foreman Fitter), A A Hester (Painter), all three won the D C Medal in The Great War. Jakeman was mentioned in 3 despatches, Golding spent 19 years in the Oxford and Bucks Territorial Force, Hester who was also mentioned in despatches, served 17 years with the King's Royal Rifles. All three were in the Bucks Special Constabulary for many years.

28 years old William Morris was killed with two colleagues in a road accident in Northern Ireland; the lorry skidded and crashed into a ditch. He had worked mainly in the wine and spirit department since leaving school.

Looking Northwards on a misty day over the top of the cask shed.

Some interesting events in the war ...

Belgian refugees were given three dozen pints of IPA per week

Thirteen pubs had slight flying bomb damage totalling £183.10s.0d in 1940.

In 1940, barricades were produced to prevent fifth columnists entering intent on sabotage.

A night watchman was employed on late duty to prevent any unauthorised persons entering.

Also in 1940, roof spotters were employed, since on one occasion working late in the brewery, loading and unloading of lorries came to a standstill after an air raid scare.

The Government requisitioned the iron railings in 1942.

The company donated £100 to the Marlow POW fund in 1942 and subscribed 100 guineas to the Marlow Fund for providing a Spitfire for Buckinghamshire.

In 1943, as a result of beer pilfering, one employee was sacked and one suspended for two weeks and two assistant drivers were demoted to being driver's mates (trouncers).

Labels shown on the right are much smaller due to the Brewery's effort to save paper.

The Stag on Easter Monday 1900; the Landlord was a Mr. Fassnidge, amongst the others are Lizzy Durrant, Polly Whitney, Mr Whitney, Bert Lilly, Jim Reeves, Ted Smith, Bill Durrant, Tommy White, and Fred 'Bussey' Derby, the dog is from the nearby Cherry Tree pub.

These two carvings hung over the door of The Shaggy Calf pub at Slough, made by F A Everatt, Priory Avenue, High Wycombe, entered in an Inn exhibition and valued at £25. The Shaggy Calf was built in 1938 but only lasted 60 years, a huge pub frequented by the Irish until they built an Irish club around the corner.

In 1906, during the felling of old Elm trees at Datchet Common, the force of strong winds caused the above accident, destroying two bedrooms. Mrs Clarke, wife of the landlord, had been lying ill but fortunately had just moved bedrooms shortly before the tree fell.

The Railway Tavern changed its name to the Jack of Both Sides in 1962. It has changed once again to a themed bar called the Honeypot. You can decide just what the theme was!

212

HONEST BEER

THOMAS
WETHERED & SONS
Brewers LTD.
MARLOW

INSPECTION of Brewery Invited

SEE HOW
PRIZE Beer and Stout
ARE MADE

*Parties taken over at 11 a.m. daily
(except Sundays).*

The last landlord was Mr. Tilbury who then moved just up the road to the Clayton Arms. Left is the original spittoon from the Queen. As can also be seen, brewery tours are nothing new. The background of the sign boards was altered from khaki to cream in 1911.

This picture shows Ted, Kate and daughter Doris in Quoiting Square, in between the Clayton Arms and The Queen. In addition to Wethered Ales, you could also buy all cooked meats and groceries here. Once Ted had retired it was taken over by Brakspear's as an off licence.

213

THE RED HOUSE AT WARREN ROW AND
THE KING OF PRUSSIA, BURNHAM BEECHES

The Red House was leased at Christmas 1905 for 21 years from Major General Micklem for £42.12s.0d per annum. In 1936, the tenant was leaving the house penniless and was granted £5 as he was destitute and 10/- a week for 3 months. The local cricket field was tucked away behind this pub.

Formerly called the Bricklayers Arms, at Burnham Beeches, it changed names to the King of Prussia, but as this name affected trade it was changed again in 1914 to the Emperor of India. However these days it has reverted back to the King of Prussia.

Note the magnificent lamp outside the Red Lion, circa 1910, and also chops and steaks on the food menu in the window. Landlord George Horton had a sideline in car hire. In the 1980's Wethered's exchanged this pub for one in Aylesbury.

The Wheatsheaf in Station Road, Marlow.

Charlie Gibbons was the last Landlord. He arrived during 1958 and was there until closure in 1960, and then he moved around the corner to the Prince of Wales.

Ken Ayres' grandfather Mr Way is centre beside Ken's mother when she was aged about five.

Thomas Way was the Landlord and before him it was his mother Charlotte, and his father Robert before that. The pub was in the Way family for well over 80 years.

1909: Mr Coleshill's father kept the Horns for 32 years and Mr Coleshill who lived with his father managed the house. On his father's death, the license was transferred to him and he has been the license holder for 22 years, so Mr Coleshill lived in the house for 54 years.

Mrs Coleshill's grandmother kept the Chairmaker's Arms, which was then known as the Jolly Harvesters. Mrs Coleshill's mother was born in that house just over 100 years ago. When Mrs. Coleshill's grandmother died, her mother took the house and carried on for some years. Fifty nine years ago, Mrs Coleshill's father and mother took the Mint and when her father died the house was taken over by her brother, Mr. T. Bowles who held the license for 40 years.

Mrs Coleshill's aunt who owned the Cherry Tree sold it to Wethered's and Mrs. Coleshill's mother was accepted as tenant so Mrs Coleshill and her mother went straight from the Mint to the Cherry Tree. Mrs Coleshill stayed at the Cherry Tree until she married Mr Coleshill and then went over to the Horns where she stayed. Mrs Coleshill claimed that her family had been tenants ever since the firm first started, Mr Coleshill was 72 years of age and suffering from asthma and Mrs Coleshill was 60 years old. Mrs Coleshill was asked whether she would like to take the Mint, but she was worried that Mr Coleshill would not live many more months. Mrs Wheeler, wife of the licensee of the Plough, is Mrs Coleshill's daughter. The Horns closed and was sold in 1972 for £72,000 and an ex gratia payment was made for outgoing tenant J. J. Clements.

The Chairmaker's Arms, The Mint and Cherry Tree were all to be found amongst the numerous pubs in Dean Street, Marlow.

The Rose and Crown landlord in the 1970s was Rex Hooker. It was later taken on by brewery assistant transport manager George 'Jock' Buchanan *(inset)*. The pub changed names a few times; it was The Eagle just before becoming an Indian restaurant. *Right:* Frank Towers, Building Manager, surveying the damage to an Austin 1100 after a wall had fallen on the car in the pub car park. *Below,* the public bar.

A nice photo of the Hare and Hounds at the bottom of Redpit's Hill, with not a house to be seen on the right along Henley Road. Wethered's tried to buy the Crown at the top of the High Street in 1933. They offered £4,000 but it was sold to Wycombe business man Frank Adams along with a firm offer of £150 per year from the adjoining Woolworth's for 42 years. He was prepared to sell the western portion back to Wethered's for the sum of £4,000 but difficulties in dividing the property made it impossible to consider in view of the high figure asked.

A fund raising function for charity at the Hare and Hounds with TV personalities Stanley Unwin and McDonald Hobley.

One of two pubs in the village, this 1930's scene includes members of the Pinches family who ran the Marlow Riding Stables in Fieldhouse Lane.

A Wethered gold lettered oak framed mirror from the 1930's.

1980s mirror.

The Yew Tree is an unusual pub, a visitor in the late 1960's would have found two rooms but no bar. You just had to sit down and someone came up and asked what you wanted to drink; then off they would go to the cellar to fetch it. Brewhouse foreman, Ray Bellamy would come up each year and trim the tree.

A cosy scene inside the Yew Tree, these customers are certainly not going to get cold.

220

THE BREWERY AND THE LANDLORD WIN THEIR APPEAL

In 1958, the brewery and landlord William Hubbick were fined £50 each for watering the whisky at The Windmill. Both denied the charges and appealed. Evidence against them was hard to prove, and the original tests proved unsatisfactory as the inspector had used the same glass six times. The fines were reduced to £10 in each case.

It was not the first time the pub has been in trouble. In 1947, the Managing Director visited The Windmill and found 14 firkins of other brewers' beers in the cellar. Also, the house and premises were in a dirty condition. He thus gave the tenant 3 months notice to terminate her contract.

Another incident in 1954, when one of the brewery draymen was attacked by the landlord's Great Dane.

Mr. Bill Hubbick and his wife Eileen.

We've got the real Holiday Spirit

Fine Old
Scotch Whisky
Alcoholic Strength 67° Proof Spirit.

THOMAS WETHERED & SONS, LIMITED,
THE BREWERY,
MARLOW.

(Controlled by Strong and Company of Romsey, Limited)

DRINKS SOLD TO BOYS IN A MARLOW HOTEL

In 1942, Monica Estelle Green, of the George and Dragon, was fined 35/- with 27/6d special costs at Marlow petty sessions. The defendant pleaded not guilty to selling intoxicating liquor to John Pauffley who was 15 years old, William Gilbert Neale, 16, Cyril Austin, 15, Arthur Webb 16, John Hobbs 16, Robert Englefield 17, and Cyril Martin 17.

Cyril Martin was fined 10/- for purchasing liquor whilst under 18, Dennis Perry was fined 7/6d for purchasing liquor for Neale, Austin and Pauffley, and Charles Glenister for purchasing liquor for Martin, Englefield, Hobbs and Webb.

Detective Constable Garrett said he entered the public bar

THERE ARE TIMES WHEN A "COPPER" WILL HELP YOU OUT!

of the hotel, and saw that some of the boys were playing darts with others sitting around a table. Noticing some of the boys were under age, he went over and told them who he was. Mrs. Ansell the landlord's wife came in and asked what was wrong and was told they were under eighteen. "Nobody asked our age, we only had mild and shandies" they claimed, but Monica insisted that they said they were over 18.

All these men were well known in Marlow.

The Ship at Marlow was leased by the William's Brewery, Wooburn, and was then taken over by Wethered's. This very rare photo taken in 1907 shows local sweep Ben Harris on top of the chimney. This photo has also appeared in the 'Best of Marlow Memories' booklet, but at that time it was not clear what was written on Ben's placard.

A newer and a bit clearer picture has now revealed it to read 'your humble servant' Two chaps are enjoying a pint in the doorway.

The Ship was bought by the tenant in 1970 for £14,500.

Ship 'B' team winners of the Rosebowl. *Back row:* J B, 'Doodle' Thorps, Landlords Mr & Mrs Arnold, Jim Munday. *Front row:* Charlie Anson, Jim Bowles, Jack Bowles Capt, Jock Ross, Fred Hook.

There was an agreement between breweries in wartime to deliver to each other's pubs in order to save fuel. The letter below was at the end of the war regarding the Clayton's return to Brakspear.

Other pubs.....

Crown, Cookham

Chequers

Coach and Horses

Crown and Anchor

Duke of Cambridge, Chalvey

Floral Arms, Slough

Hand and Flowers

Horse and Groom, Penn

Jolly Farmer, Cookham

Wendover Arms,

High Wycombe

Walnut Tree, Bourne End

There was an exchange of trade with both Simond's in 1941 and Chesham Brewery in 1943.

The Britannia was one of the last public houses to be built in Marlow. The landlords in 1961 were Mr and Mrs J. Valentine. Their joint weekly salary was £11.3s.6d. *Inset, left to right:* HH Palmer, Paul Thompson and A. Coventry looking at plans for the first Wethered House to be built since 1938

"THE SHITEHAWKS"

Following a dispute between the members of the darts team in the pub, they split into two sections, one moving into the back room and calling themselves 'The Shitehawks' just to be awkward! in the above picture they are off on an outing. Some of the names.....Ray Sparks, Doug Carter, Dave Stevens, Larry Ludgate, Jack Dent, Alf Gloucester, 'Sunner' Stone, George Carter, 'Whippet' Wakefield, Bob Tuffrey, John Pauffley, Bill Devereux, Bert Bunker, Jack Hammond, Ron Flint, Ray Carter.

Photos taken in December 1984 when a new pub sign was unveiled at the Two Brewers. Signwriter, Ken Mansfield and Company Chairman, Sam Whitbread are seen talking to Mrs Wethered. Far left is the Mayor, Councillor Maurice Oram. The sign shows Thomas Wethered, but on the other side of the sign it shows Whitbread company founder Sam Whitbread.

Standing, Bob Martin with two of his children Glenys and Ann. Sitting next to them is their grandad, Walt Randall.

Owing to the huge success of Wethered bitter in London pubs, in 1988 the company decided to refurbish the Red Lion in Rosoman St, Clerkenwell costing £150,000 and called it The Thomas Wethered. It did not last too long and after experiencing a few name changes and themes, it is now the A La Cruz Latin American restaurant.

The Whip at Lacey Green, an excellent pub for real ale lovers, as it also hosts a few beer festivals each year. In the field behind is a windmill dating back to around 1650 and since 1971 has been restored to working condition by The Chiltern Society.
Below, a cellar typical of the 1950's

An annual event was the Wethered flower competition open to all Wethered pubs. It was judged by Frank Towers (builder's manager) and 'Jock' Seaton. One of the most successful pubs was The Greyhound at Peppard now owned by celebrity chef Anthony Worrel Thompson.

Ernie Wise and Bryan Humphrey, the Managing Director, they made a great double act. It was Bryan's idea to have a brewery family day.

Ernie Wise, with no chance of starting that!

Ernie Wise and Bryan Humphrey looking as if they are going to sing a duet. A new double act – Humphrey and Wise.

A commemorative plate was presented to all who attended.

Above: Keith Budd, Jack Frost, Ron Climpson, Mike Holliday, Bryan Humphrey, Ernie Wise, Lesley Tunney, Dennis Woods, Tony Wilkinson and Tim Millbank.

Something for all the family.

Vintage lorries on show, alongside 38 ton ERF

Budding photographer, assistant transport manager, Melvyn Deri.

Managing Director Bryan Humphrey is looking the wettest.

Dennis 'two dinner' Woods was the most popular person to soak.

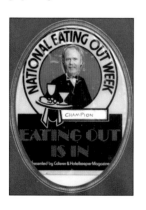

Mick Mitchell winning the ale drinking competition.
We wonder why!

Yes, my mum said I could pick the cement out of the wall if I want!

Ernie Wise and Bryan Humphrey cracking a few jokes.

Guess the weight of the Whitbread Shires?

A Showman's traction engine on display in the top yard.

You can trust Ken
'Shadow' Bowles to be
behind the wheel.
He wouldn't be doing the
pulling.

Some of the others
pulling are: David Lee,
Glyn Pounds, John
Brainch

Cutting up the old copper which was originally coal fired.

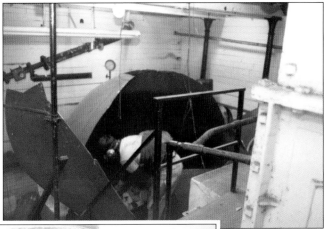

With a section cut away it is just possible to see the heater.

999, Fire and Ambulance!

The sort of thing that can happen when you cut things up in a confined space: one of the scrap men cutting in a tank with a petrol cutting machine passed out due to the fumes. Two draymen, John Brainch and Claude 'Lummy' Deane, dragged him out and he was taken to hospital.

The sad sight of an empty fermenting room after the scrap men had been let loose.

This is where the copper was situated.

All that was left of the yeast press.

There goes the garage.

Here lies the
carpenter's shop

Next job was to fill in
the cellar.

DEMOLITION REVEALS AN EXCITING ARCHAEOLOGICAL DISCOVERY

When the dust finally settled on the remains of the cellar service department, an archaeological team moved in. The discovery was of a medieval building, almost certainly an Inn, could it be the 16th century Inn the Three Tuns Tavern? It seems only fitting that the Hogshead pub was built on this exact site, although it is now named the Slug and Lettuce. To the rear, Little Stone House can be seen: Solicitor's offices for many years, but now one of the town's many boutiques.

Labels *above* were when Wethered's merged with Strong's.

At the back of Remnantz a croquet lawn.